AF480176

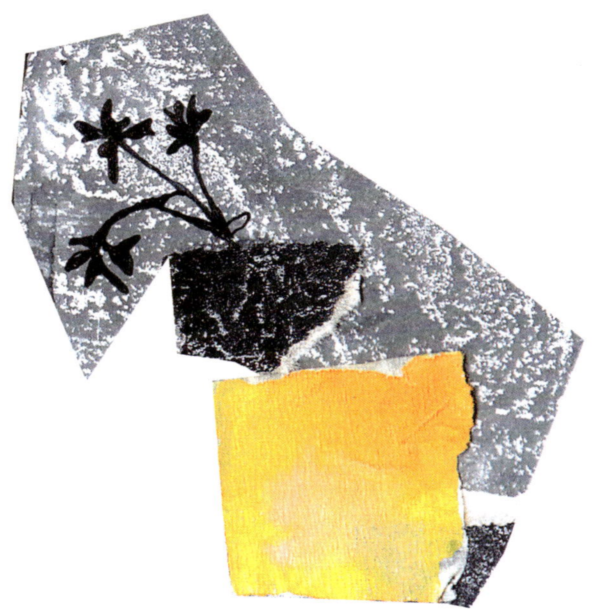

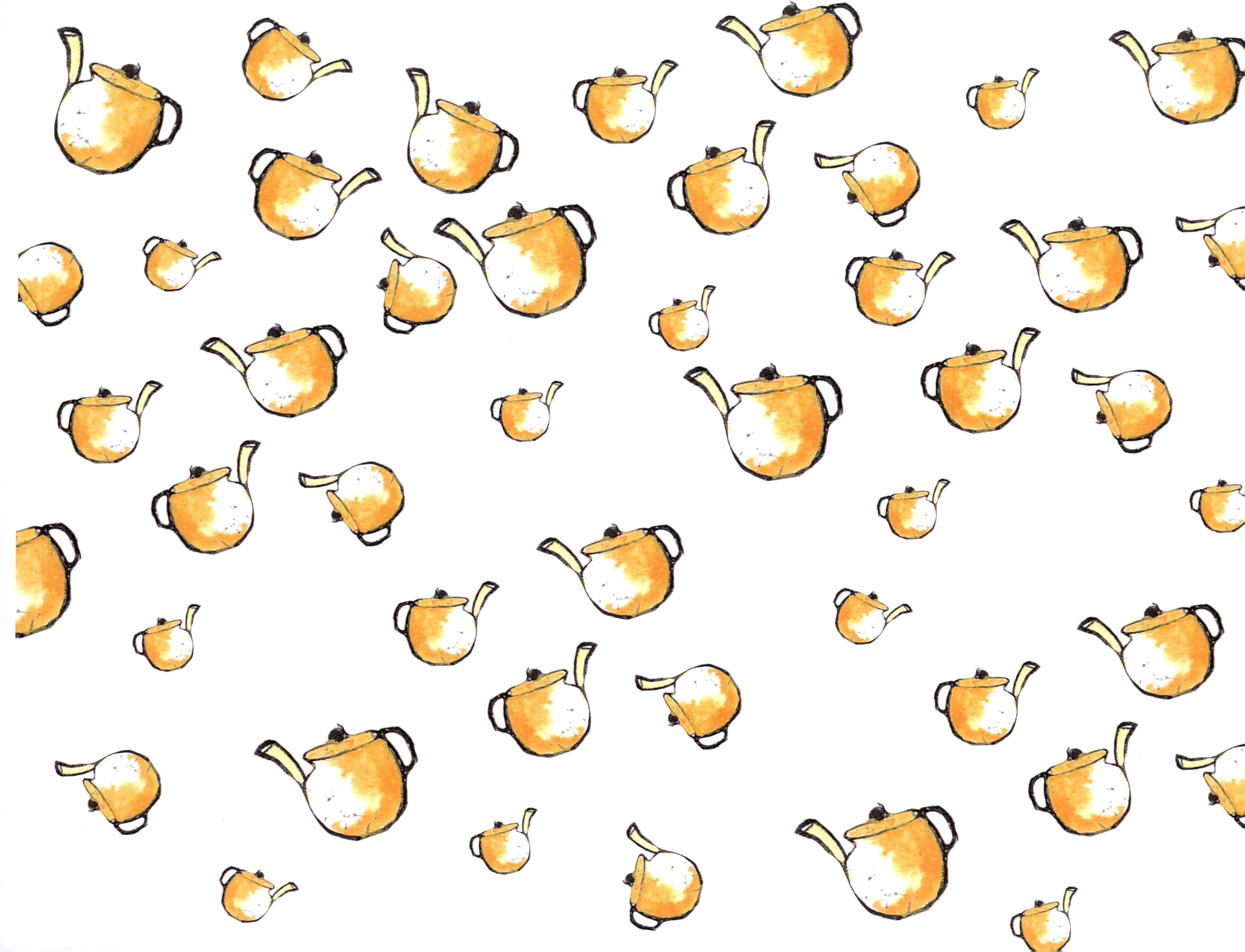

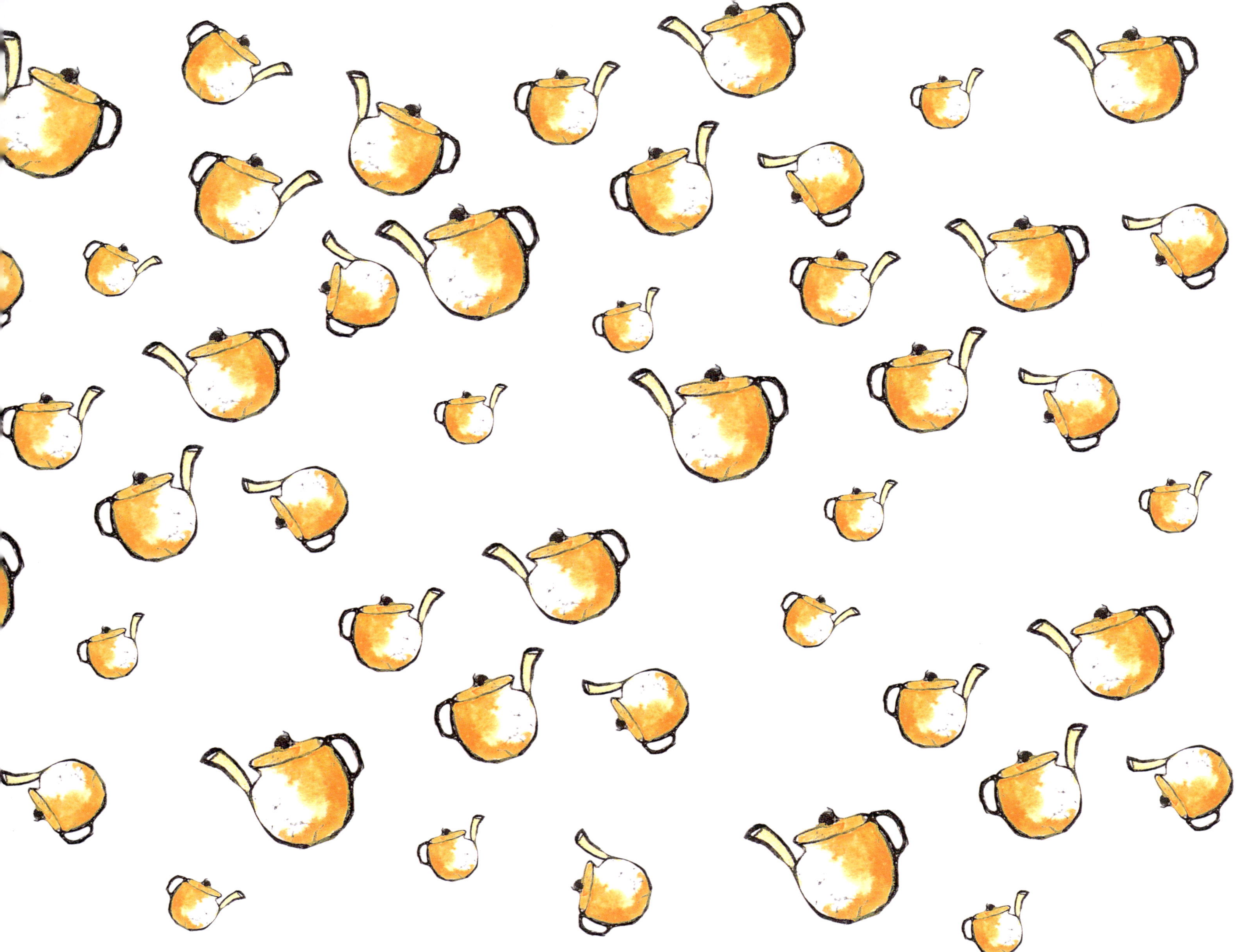

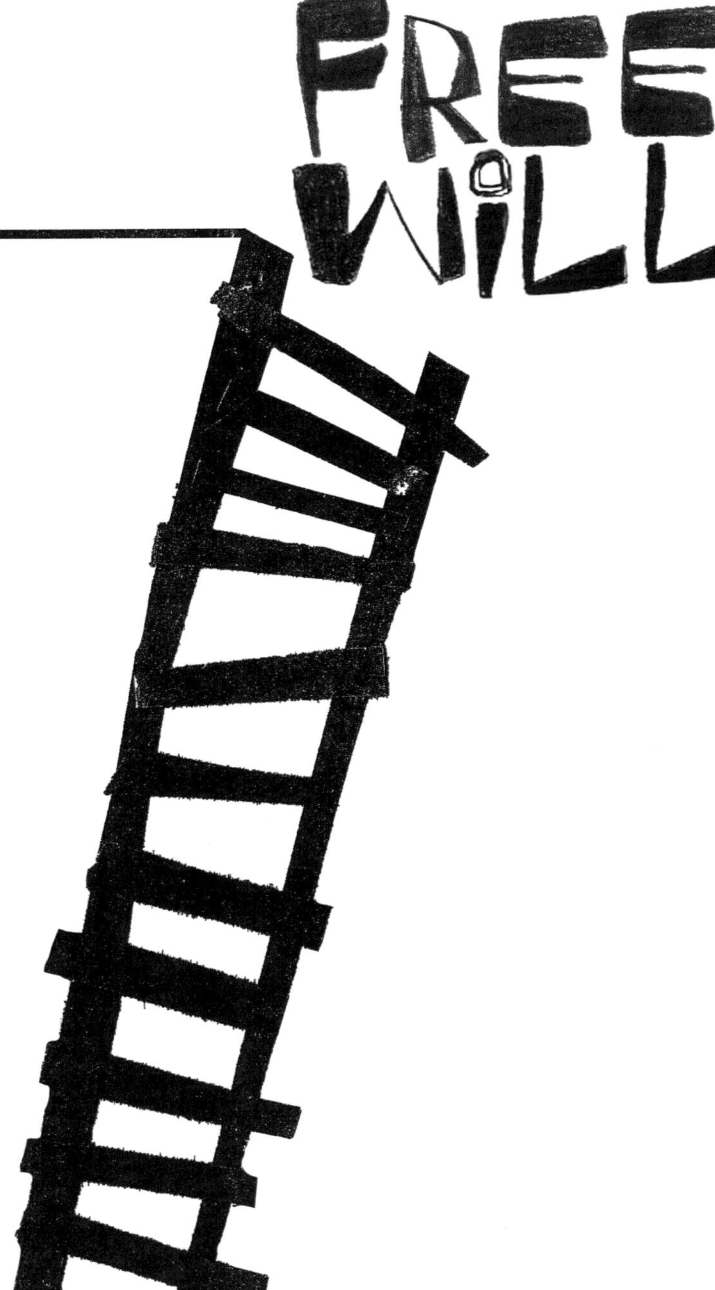

FREE WILL
BAHAR TAGHIANI

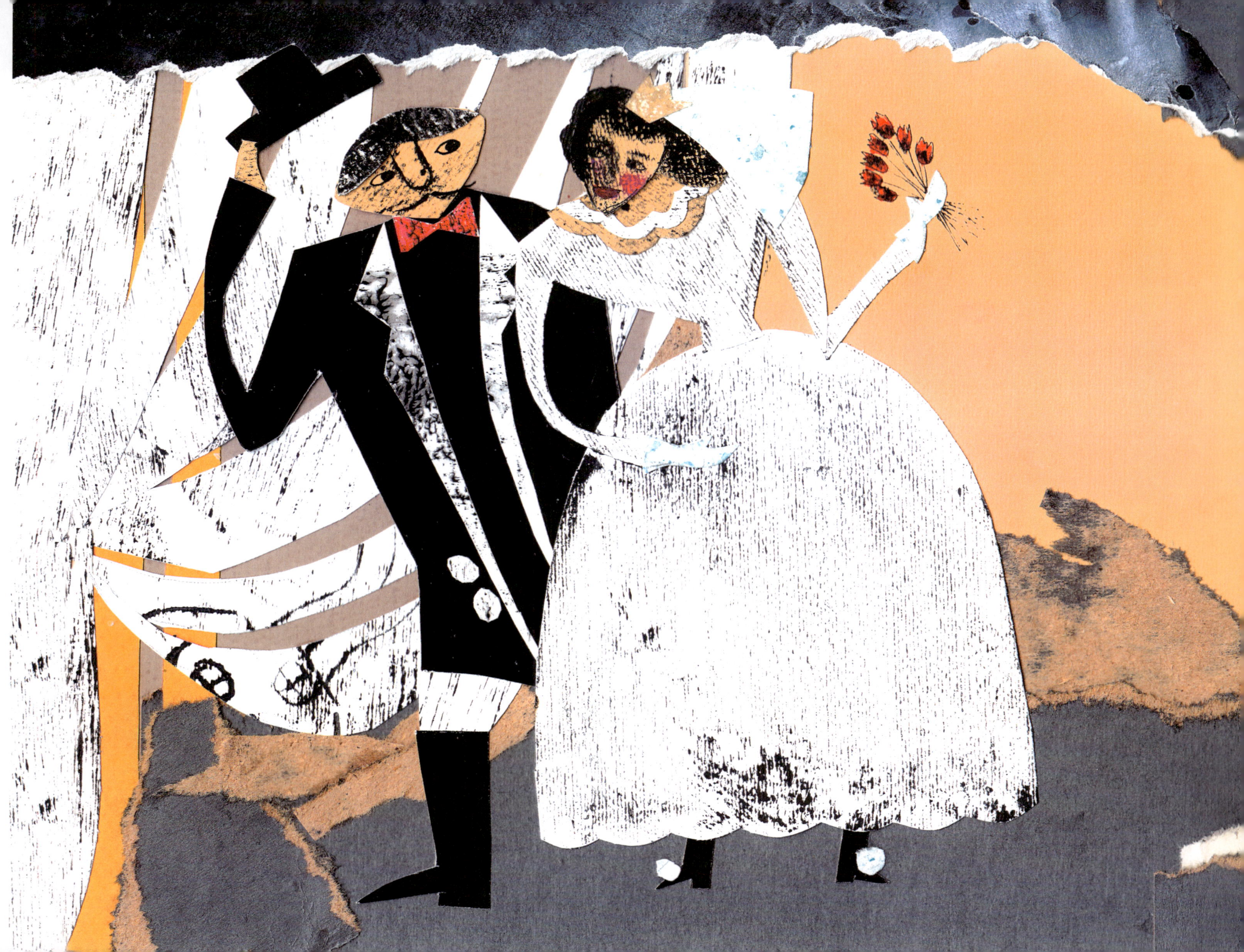

THE GIRL IS MARRIED.

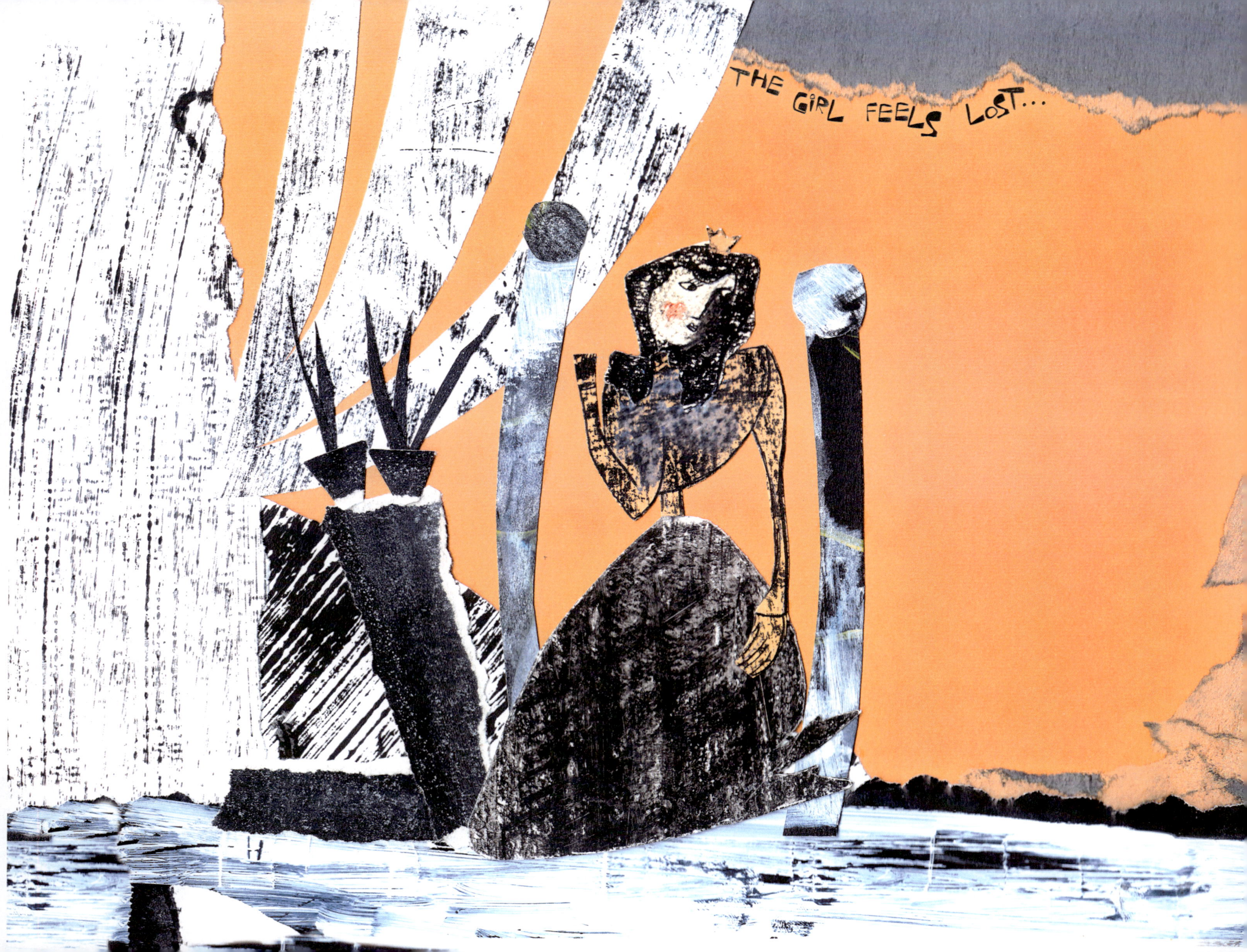
THE GIRL FEELS LOST...

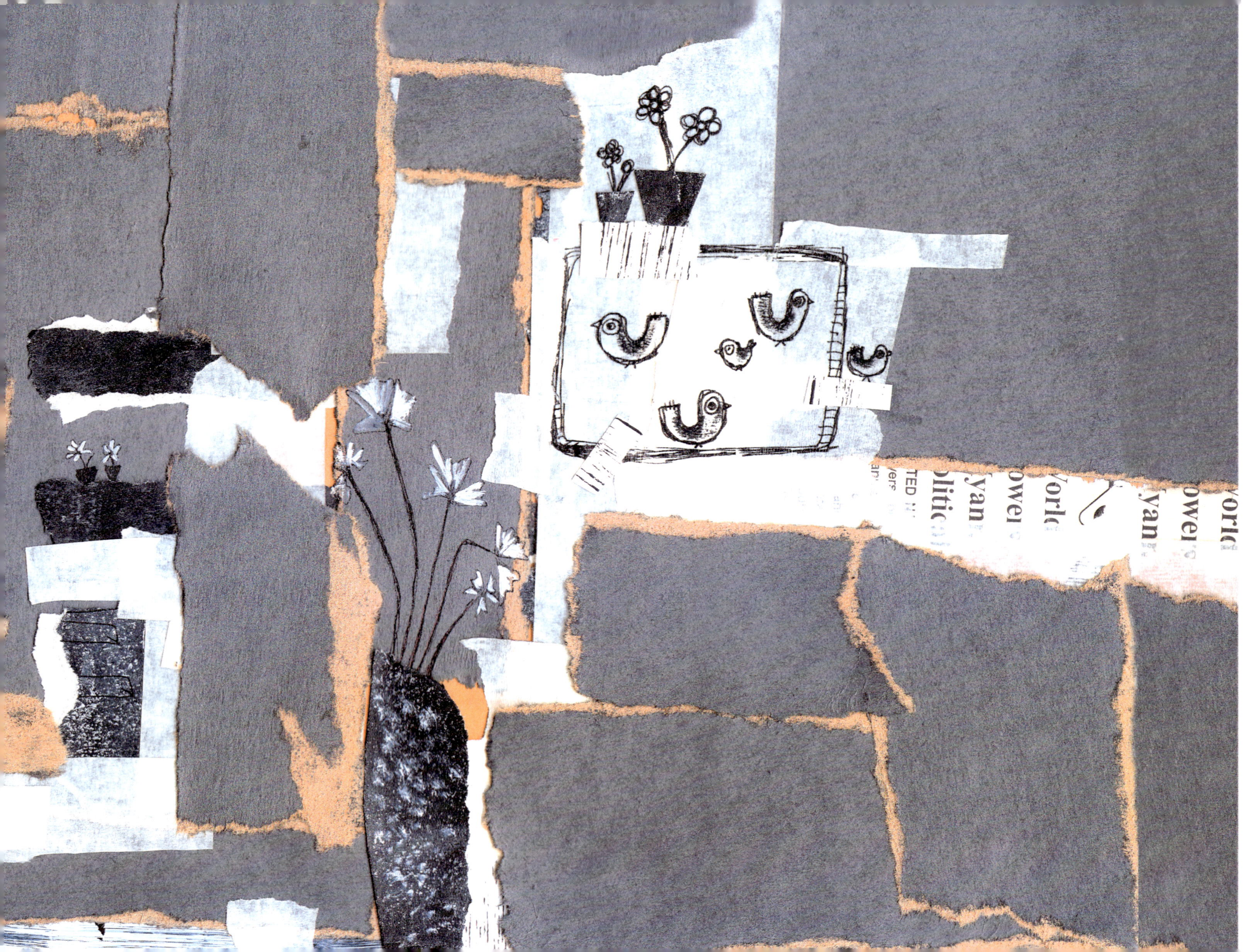
orld
owei
yan
World
owe
yan
olitic
TED

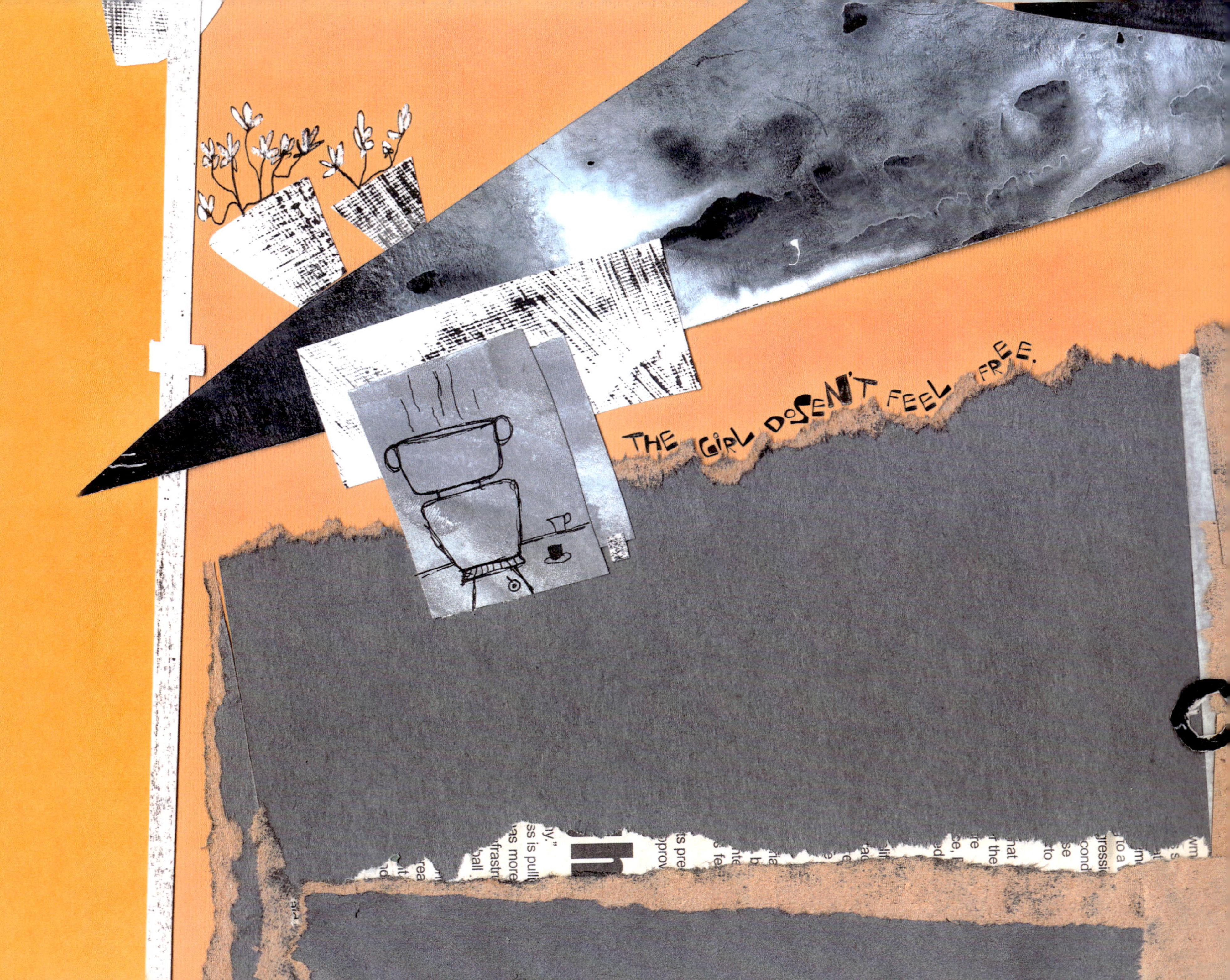
THE GIRL DOSEN'T FEEL FREE.

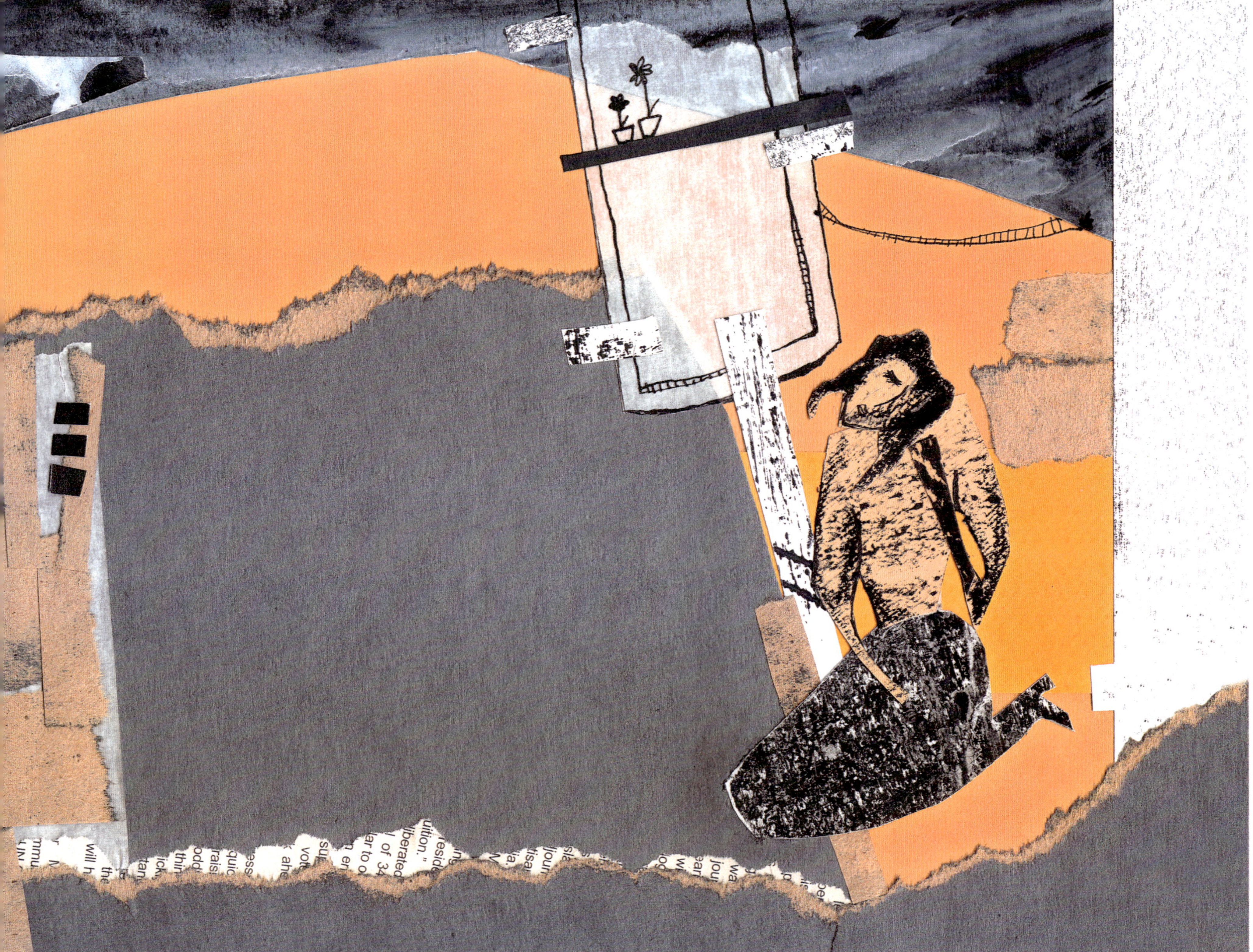

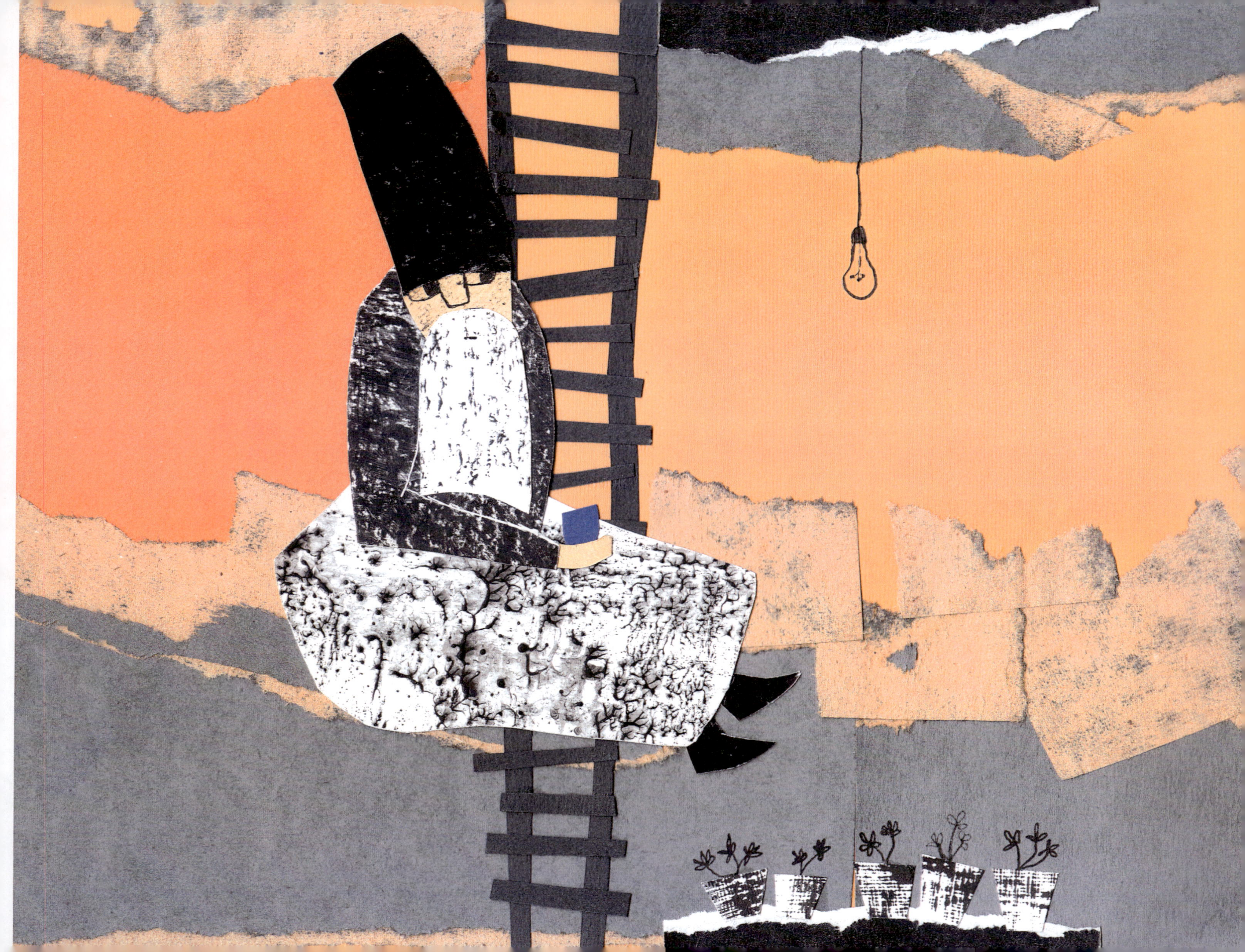

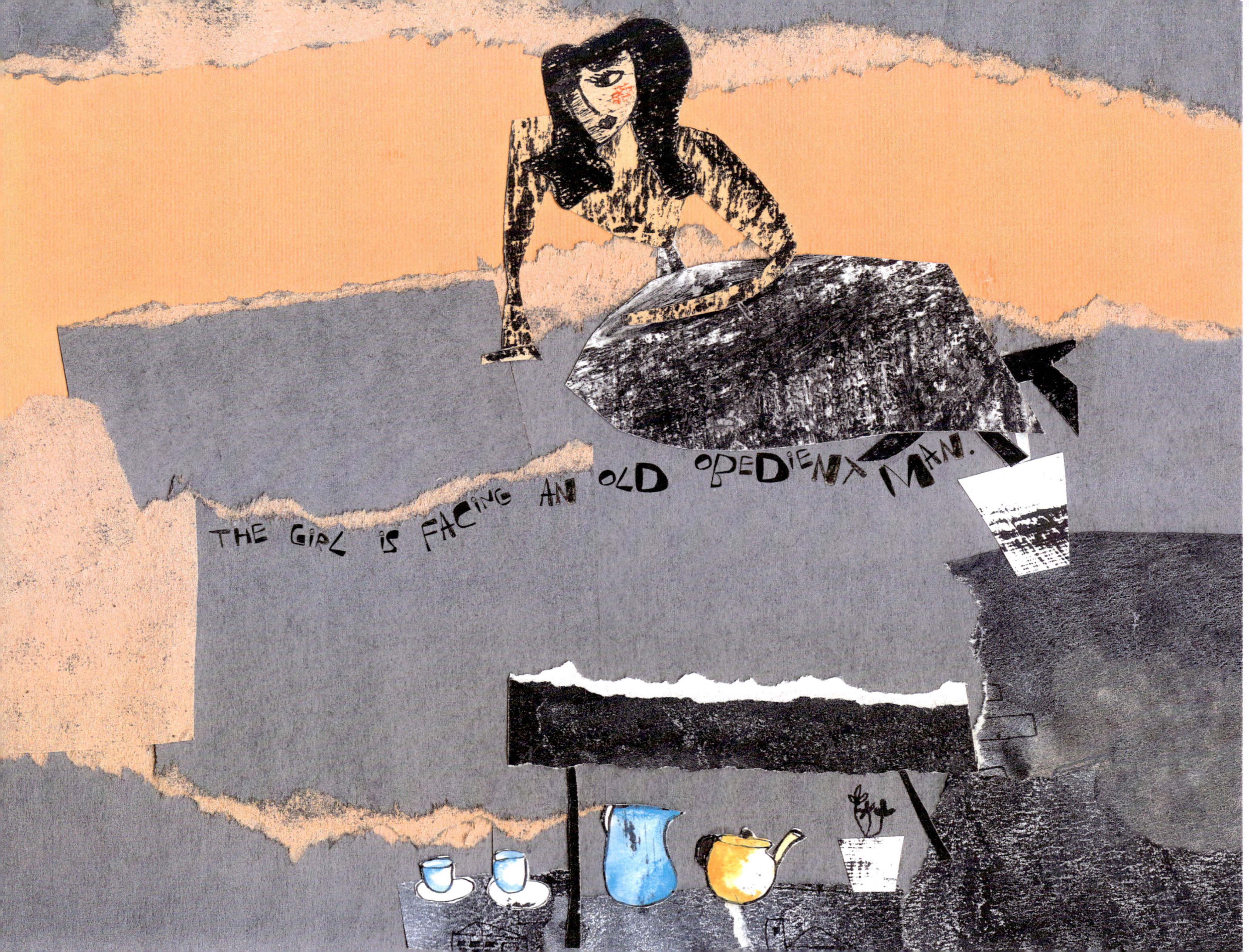
THE GIRL IS FACING AN OLD OBEDIENT MAN.

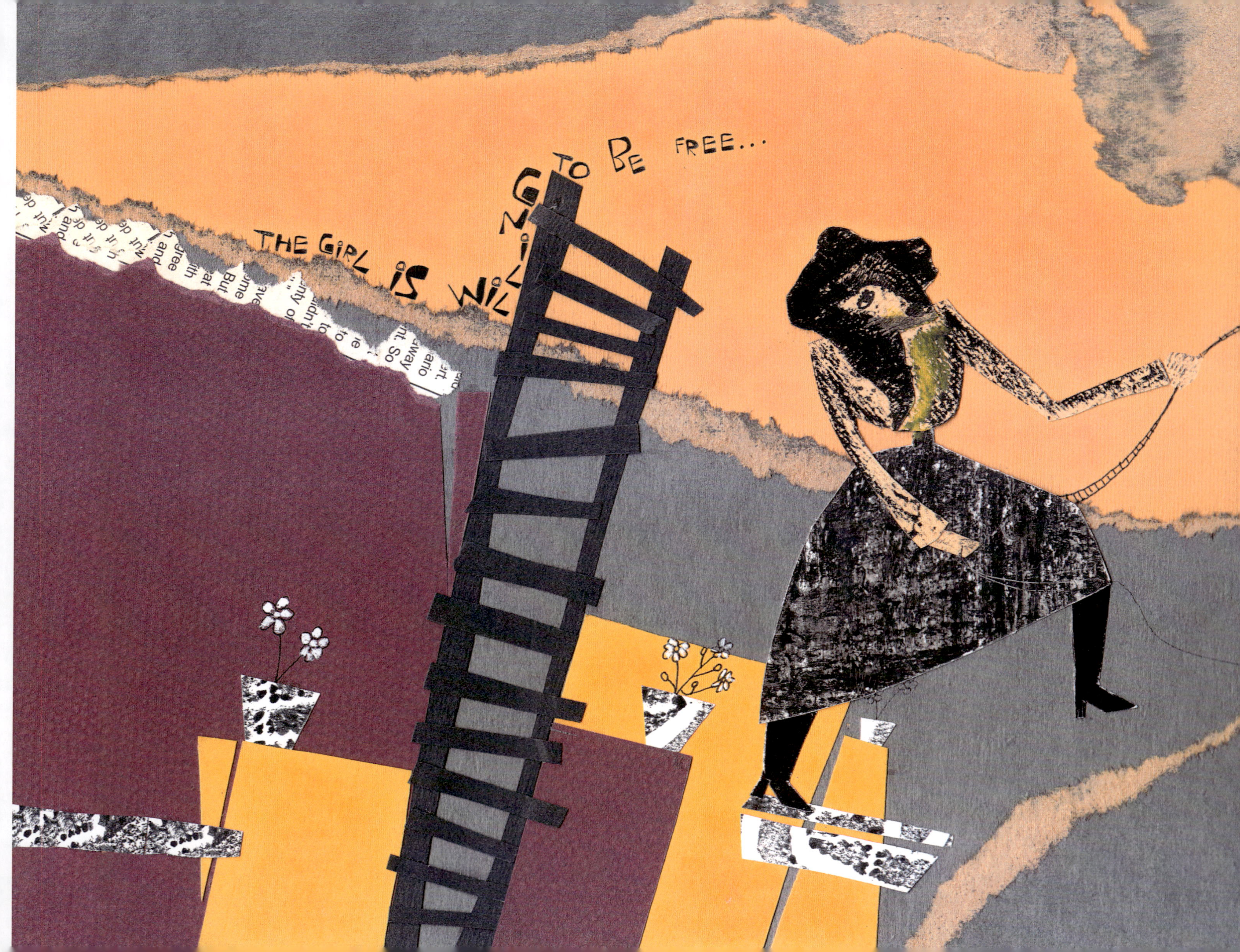
TO BE FREE...
THE GIRL IS WIL
G
TO

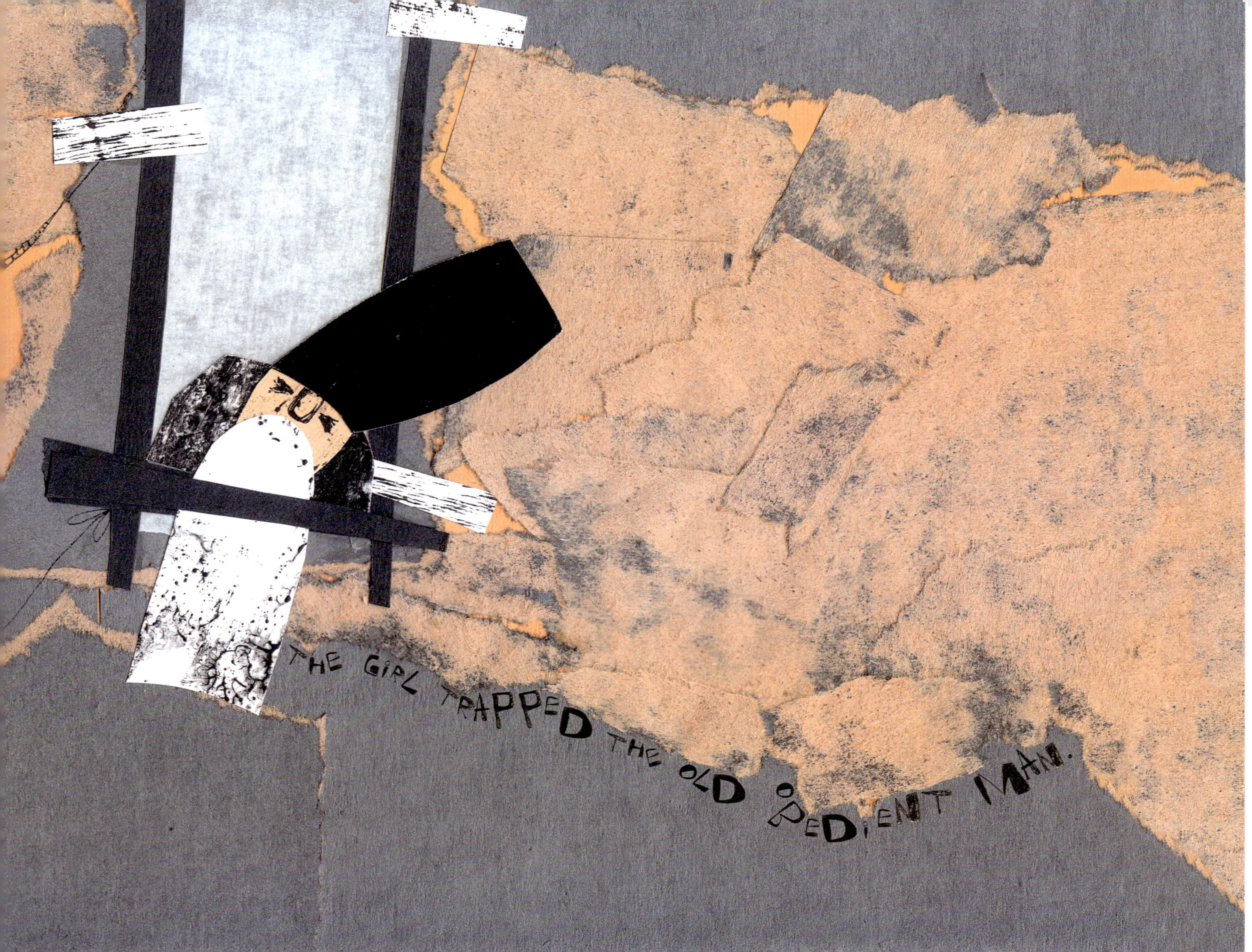

70
THE GIRL TRAPPED THE OLD OBEDIENT MAN.

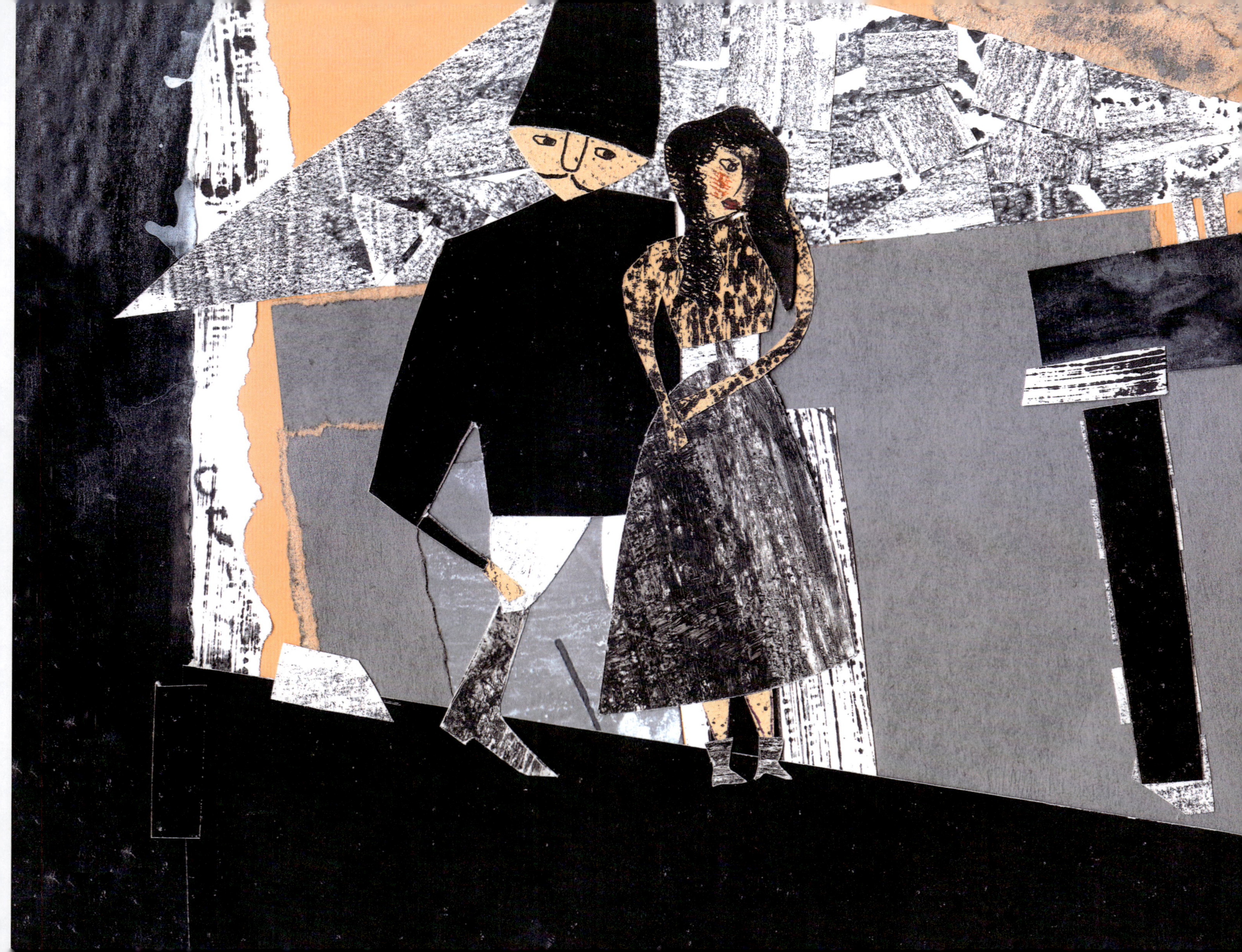

THE GiRL iS ACCoMPANYiNG A YOUNG MAN OF FEAR.

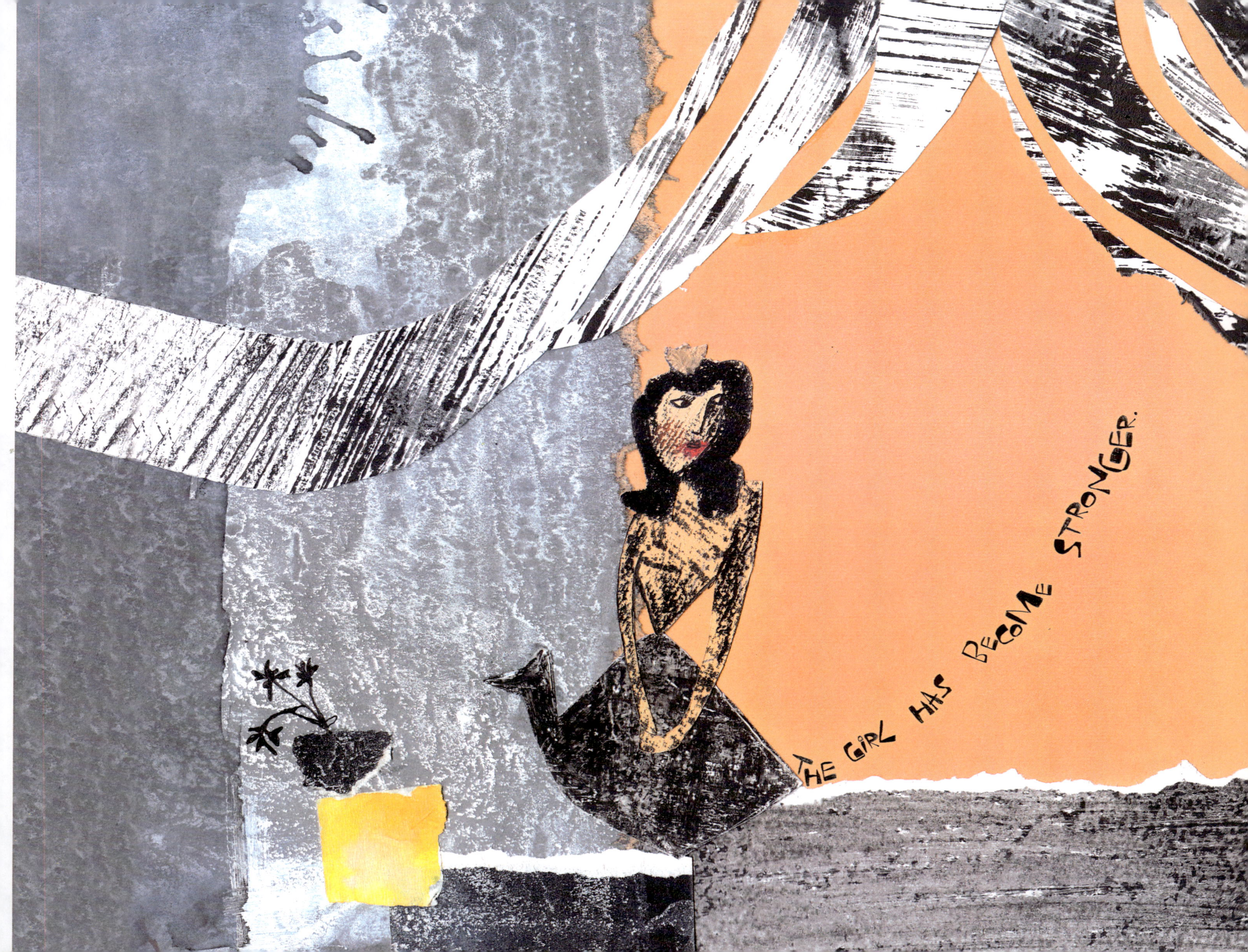

THE GIRL HAS BECOME STRONGER.

SHE ASSOCIATES WITH THE KING OF COURAGE.

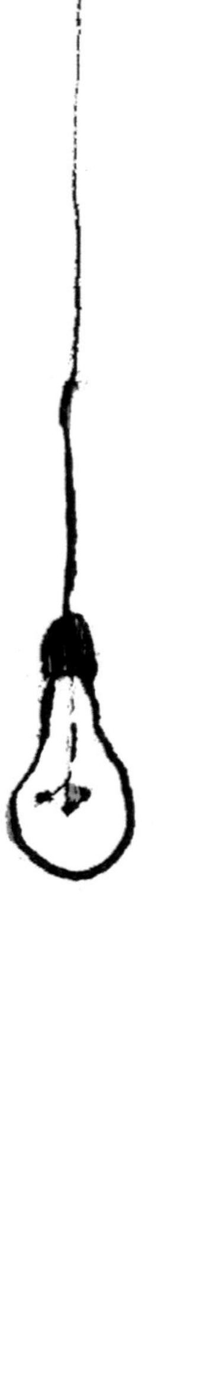

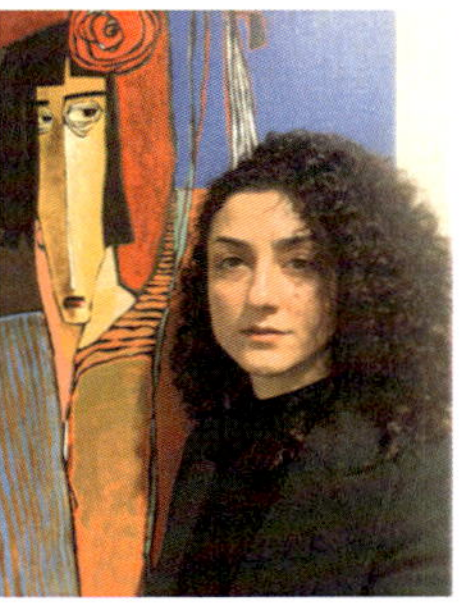

Bahar Taghiani is an illustrator and visual artist whose love for visual imagery began in early childhood. She started by creating characters out of pieces of paper, placing them in imagined stories, and bringing them to life. Today, her artworks are primarily created using mediums such as acrylic, collage, colored pencil, and watercolor, drawing inspiration from her perception of the world around her. Bahar is an award-winning artist, recognized by UNICEF for her illustration in the competition "Children on the Eve of New Year."

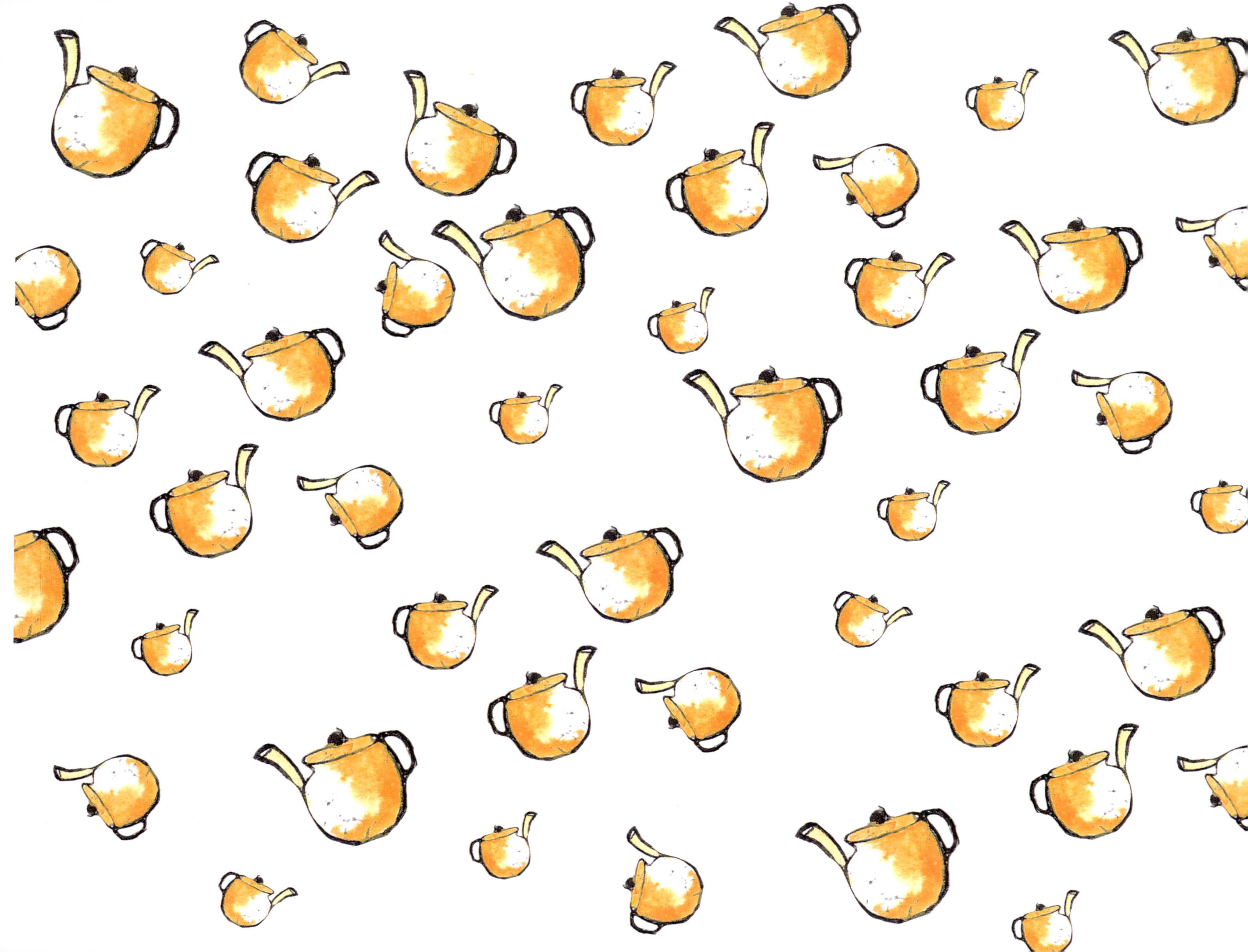

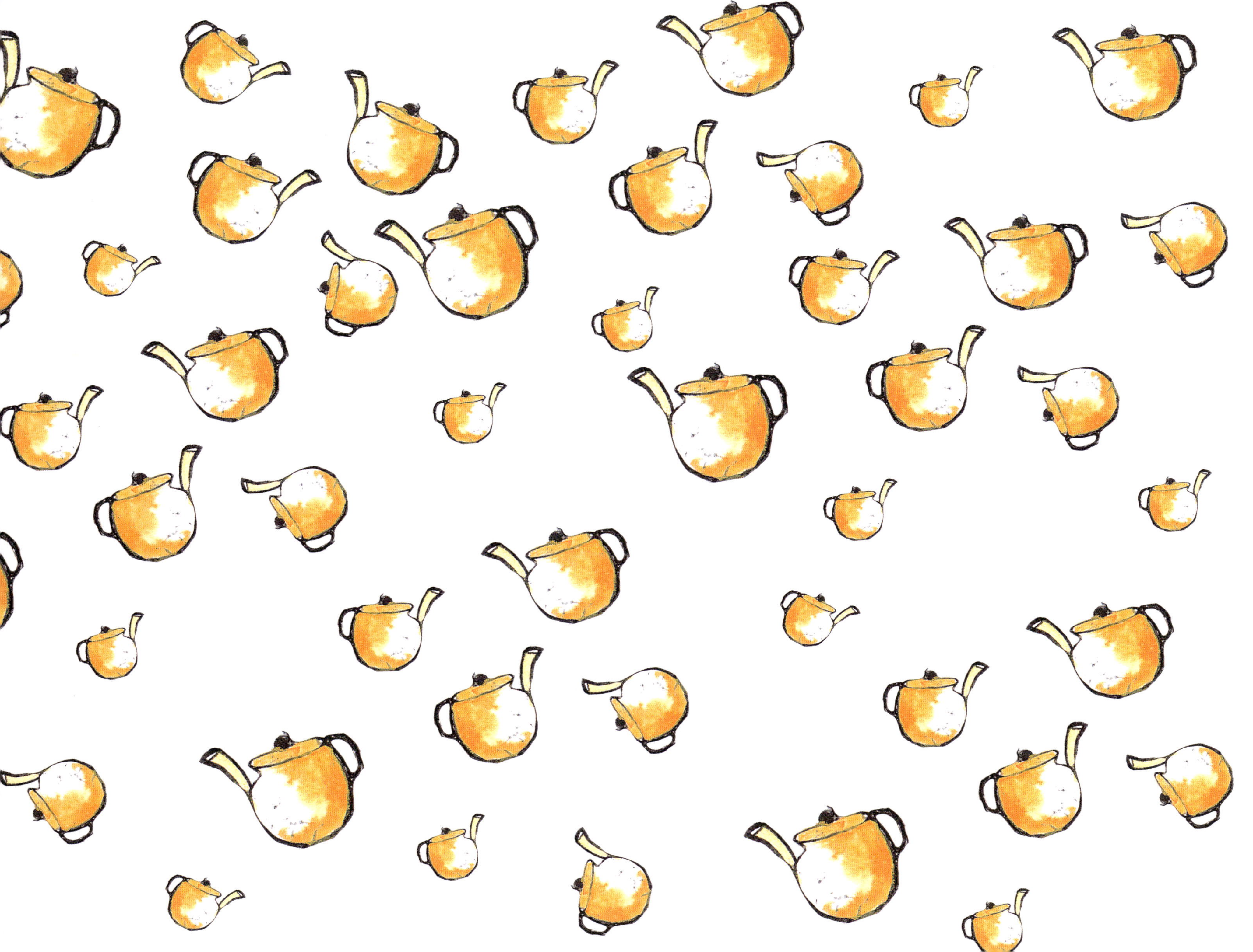

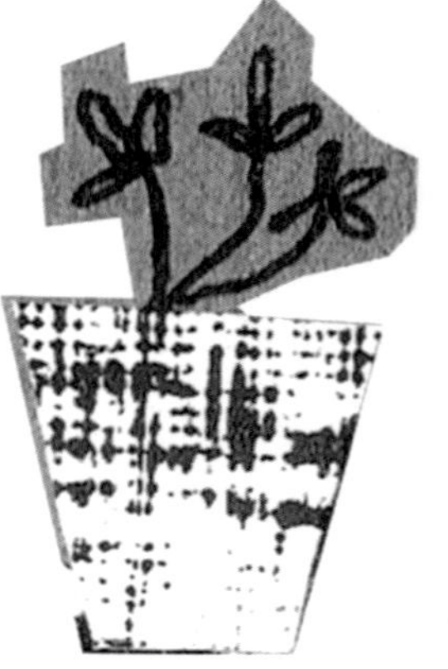

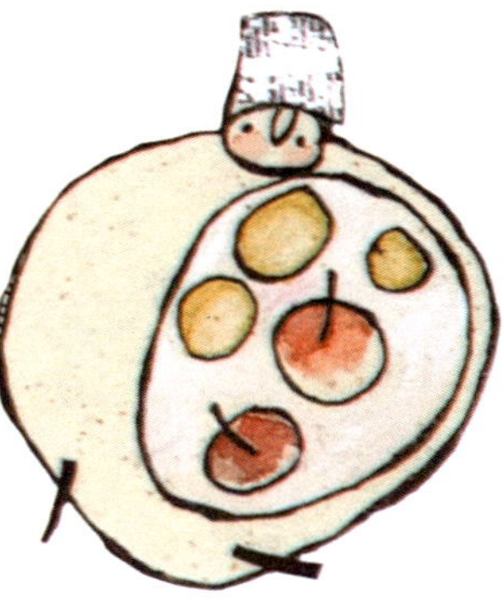

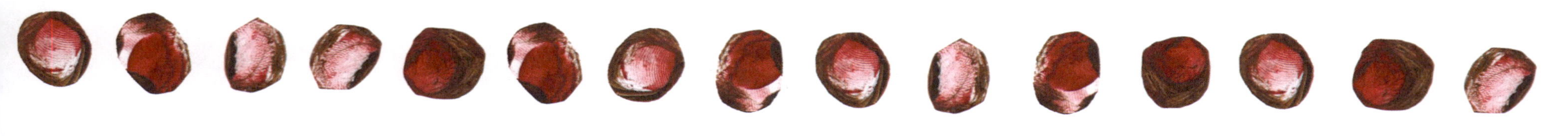

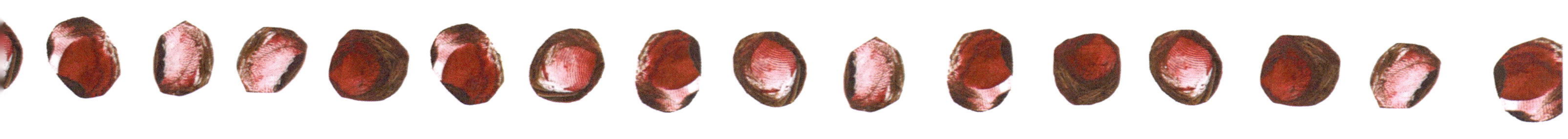

SEWING WOMAN

BAHAR TAGHIANI

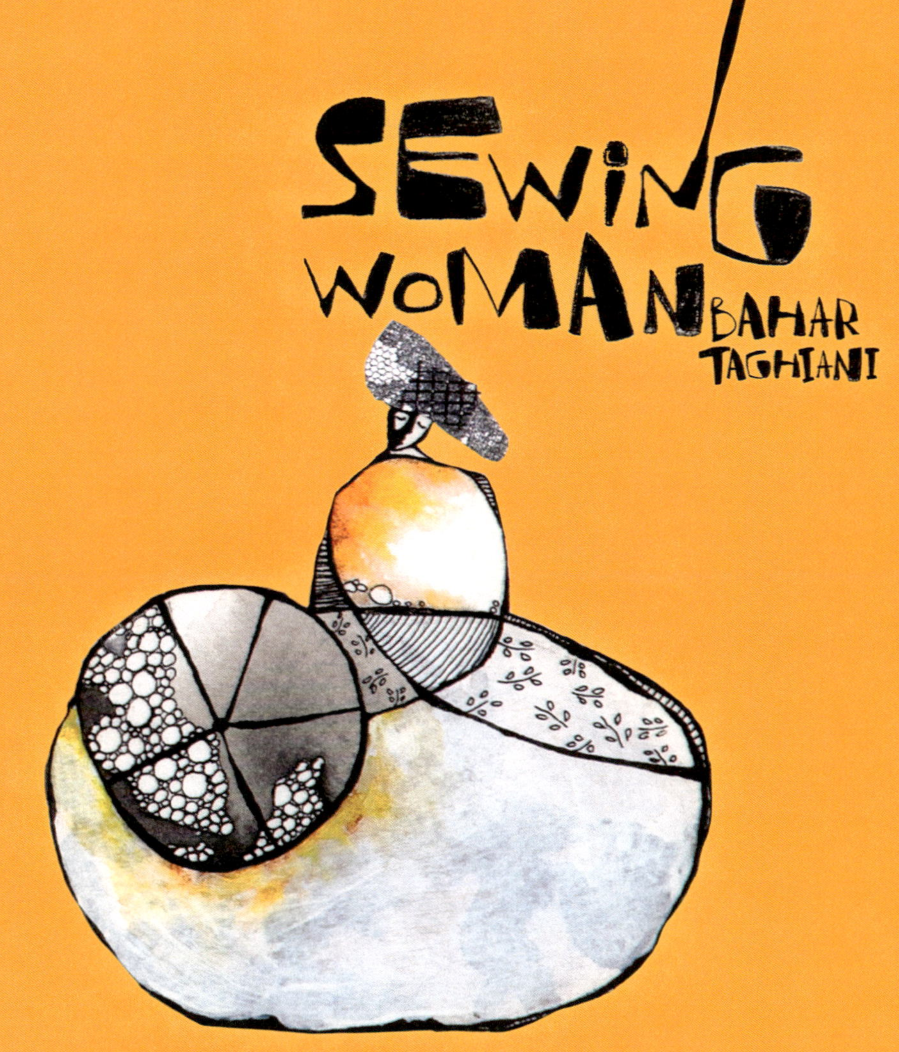

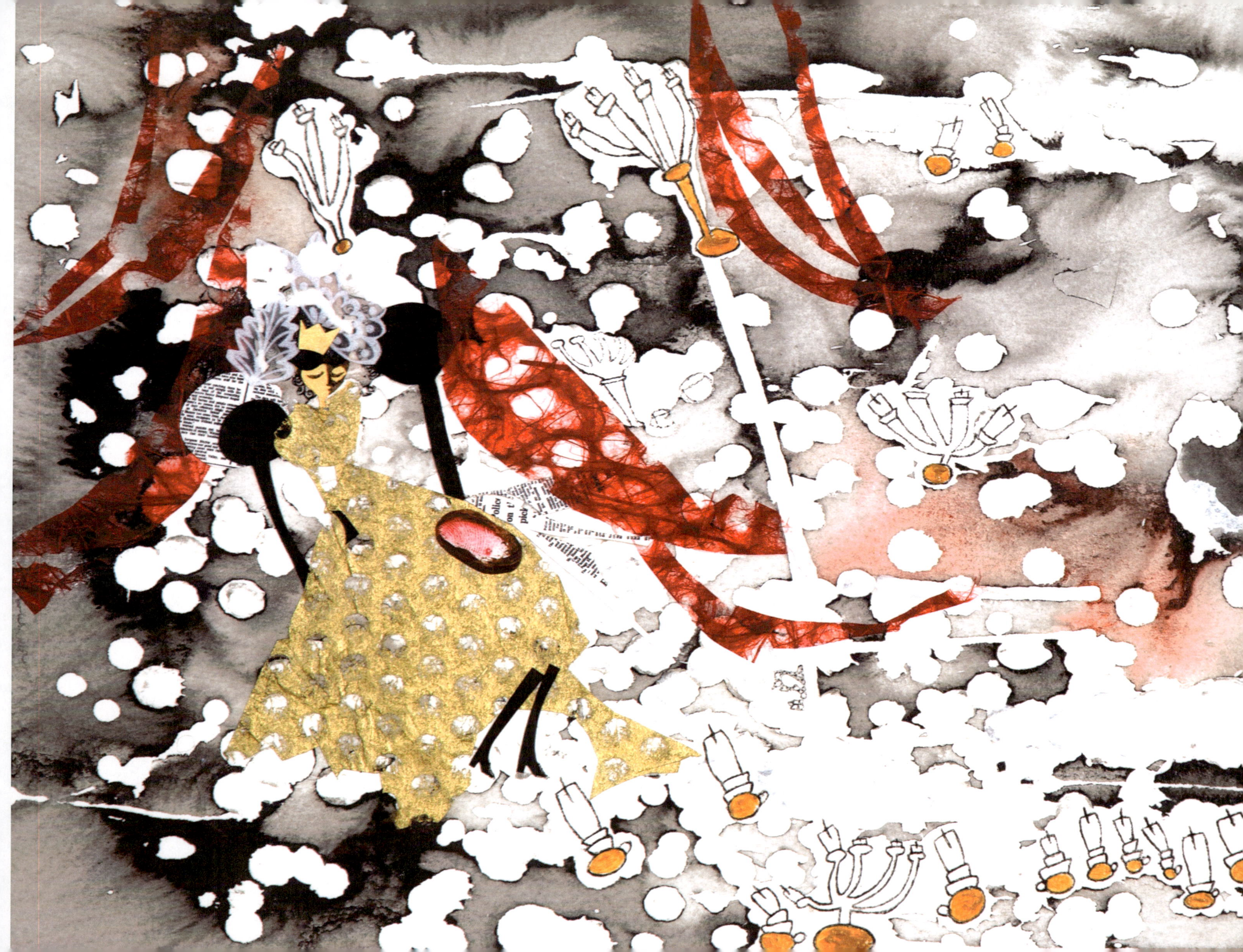

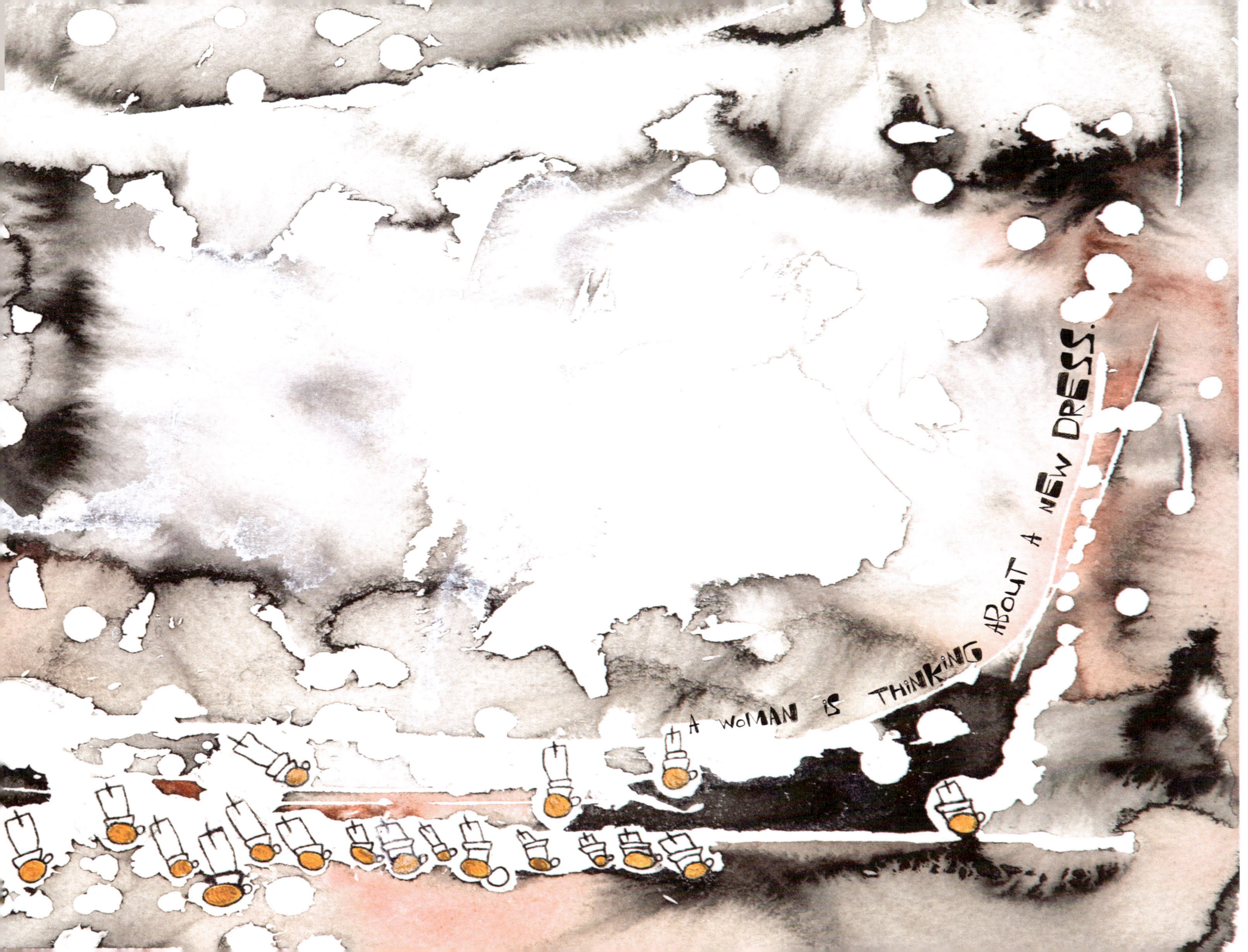

A WOMAN IS THINKING ABOUT A NEW DRESS.

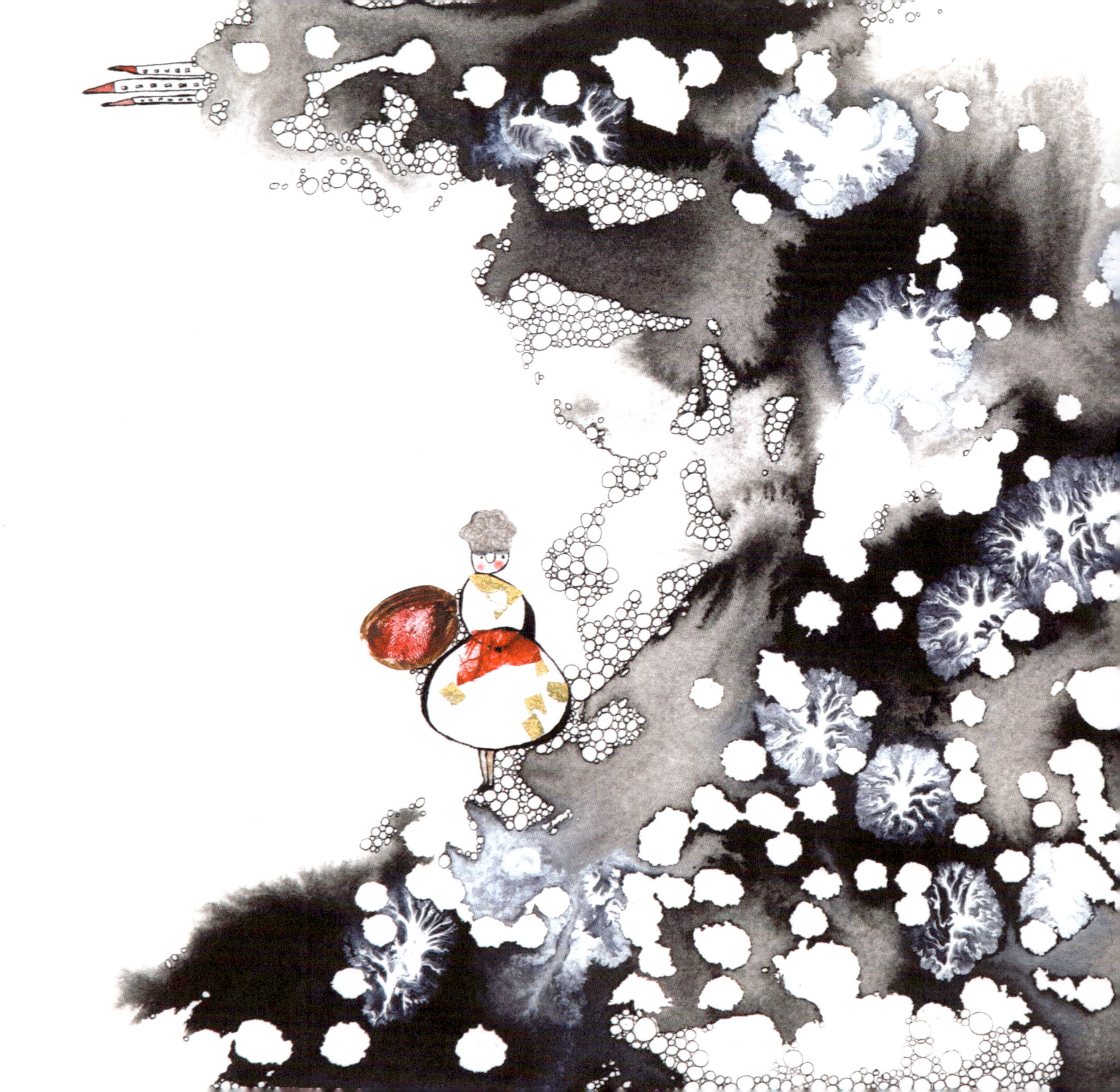

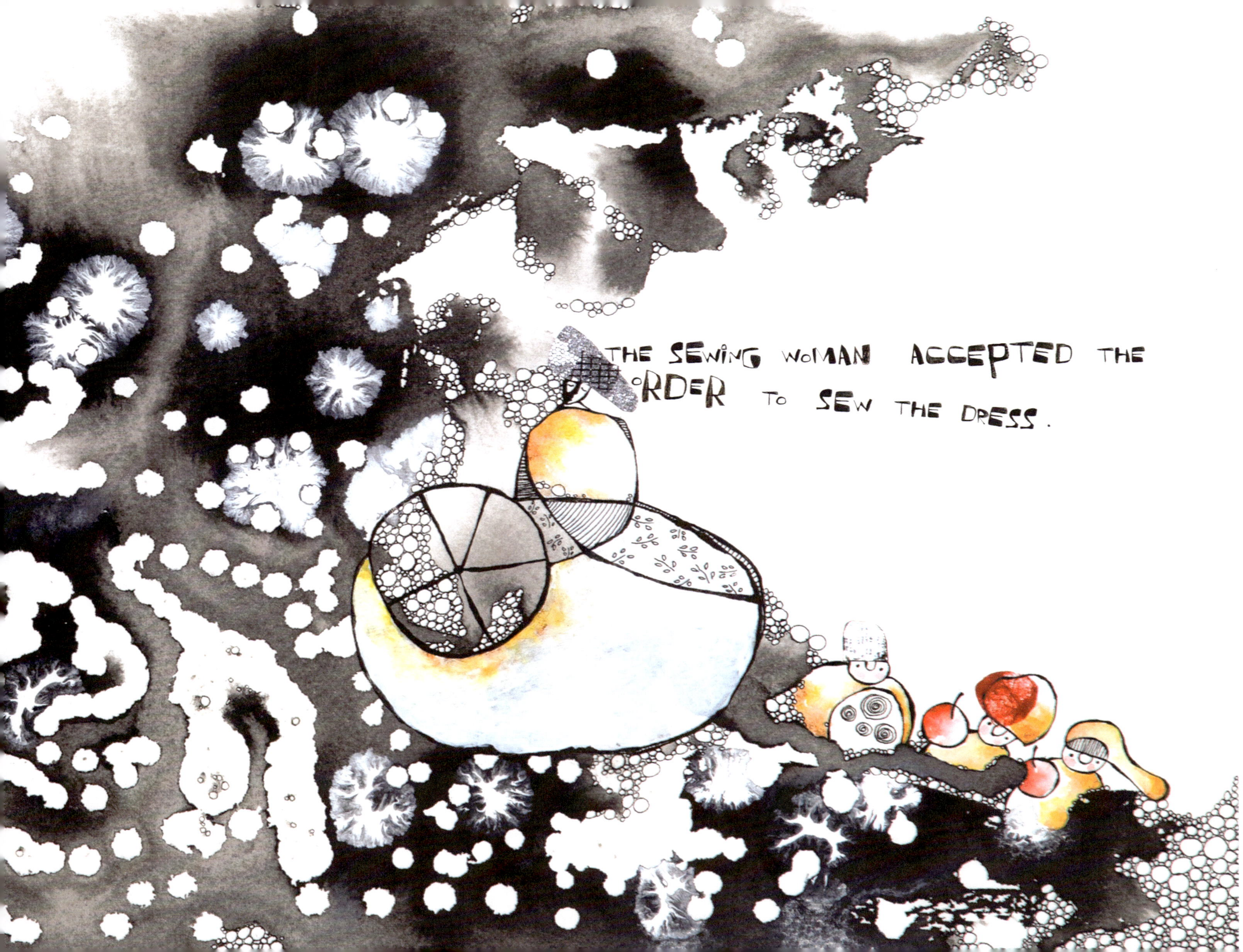
THE SEWING WOMAN ACCEPTED THE
ORDER TO SEW THE DRESS.

THE SEWING WOMAN IS GOING TO THE
FABRIC MARKET WITH THE KIDS.

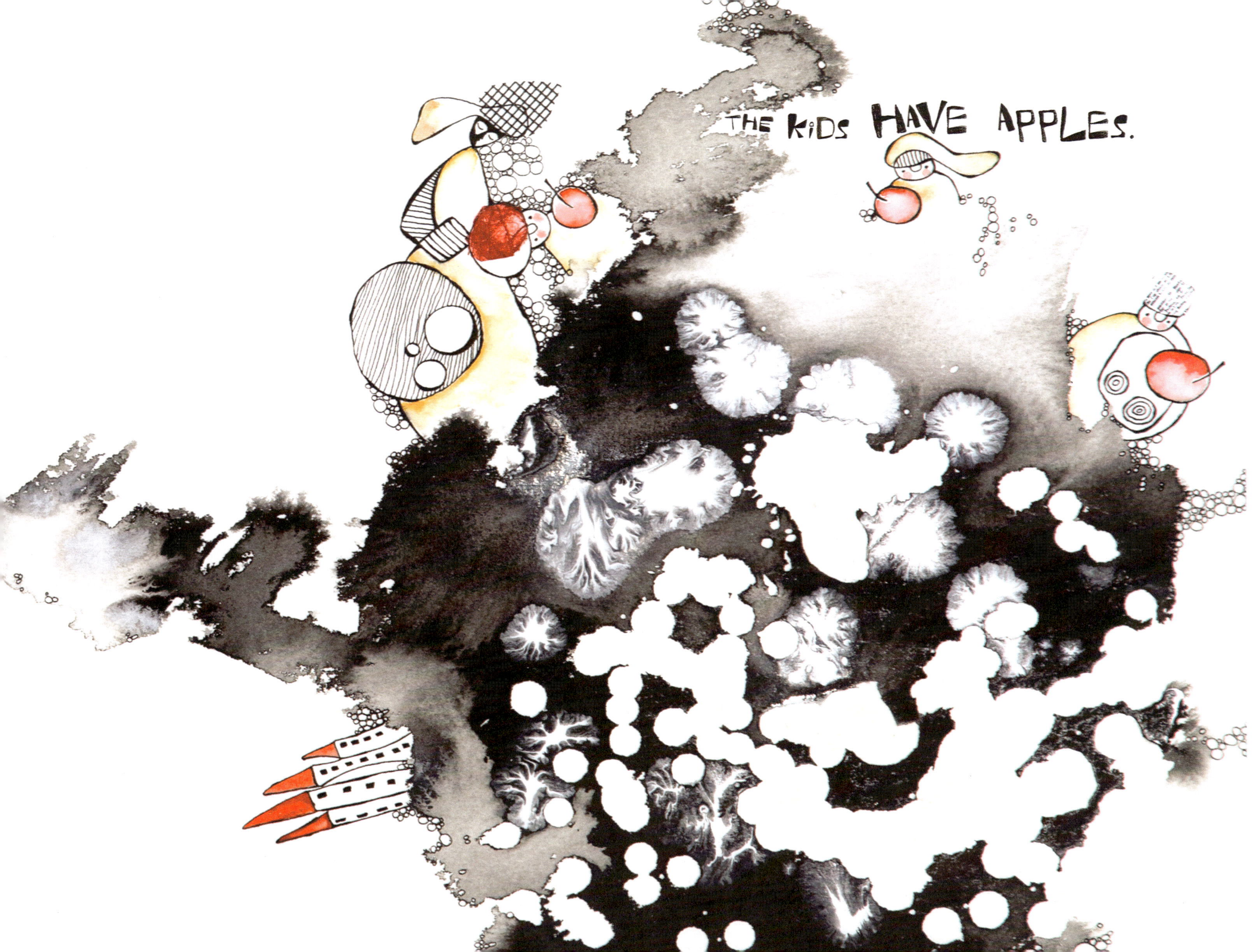
THE KIDS HAVE APPLES.

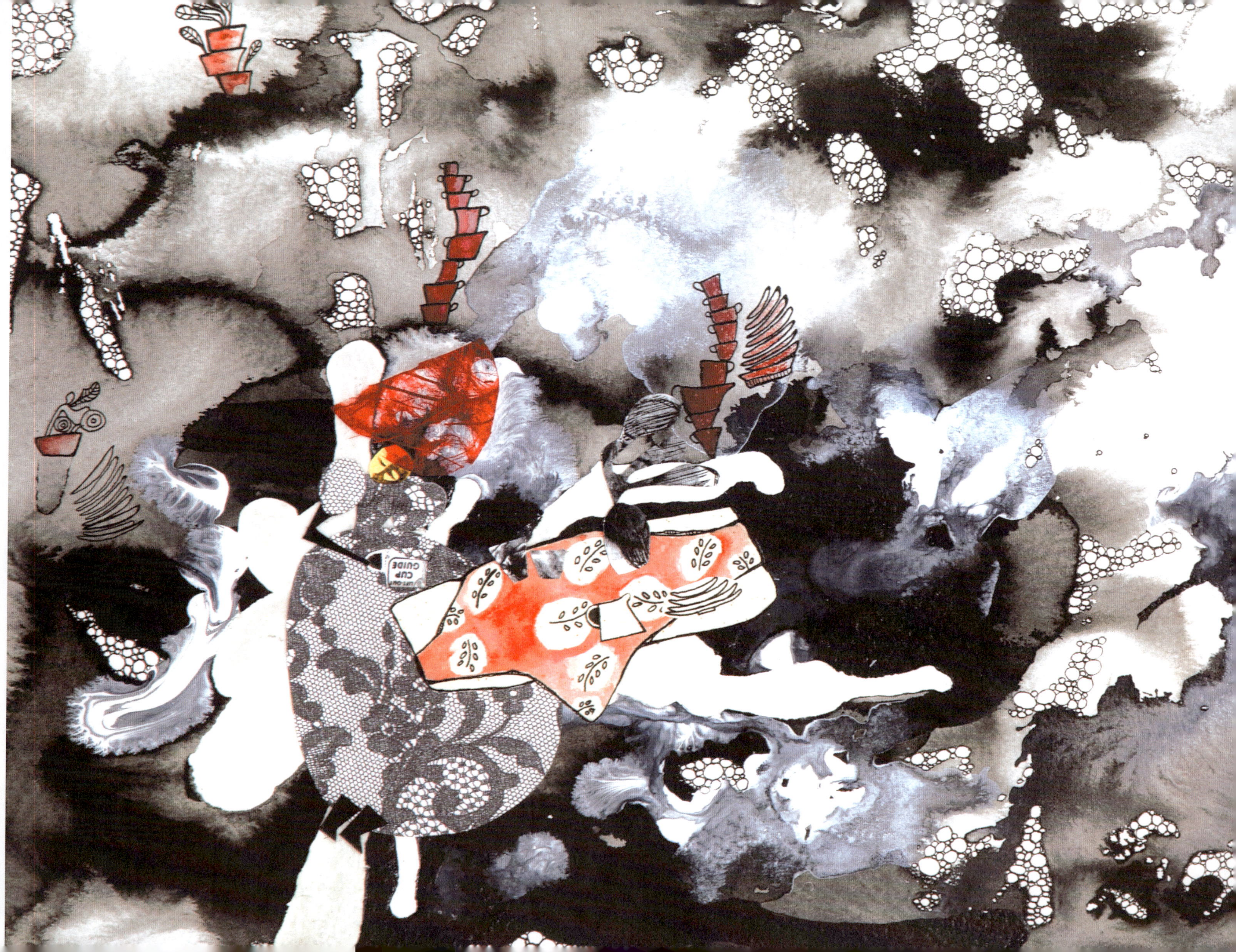
CUT OUT
CUP GUIDE

THE WOMAN WENT TO THE SEWING WOMAN'S HOUSE
TO GET HER DRESS.

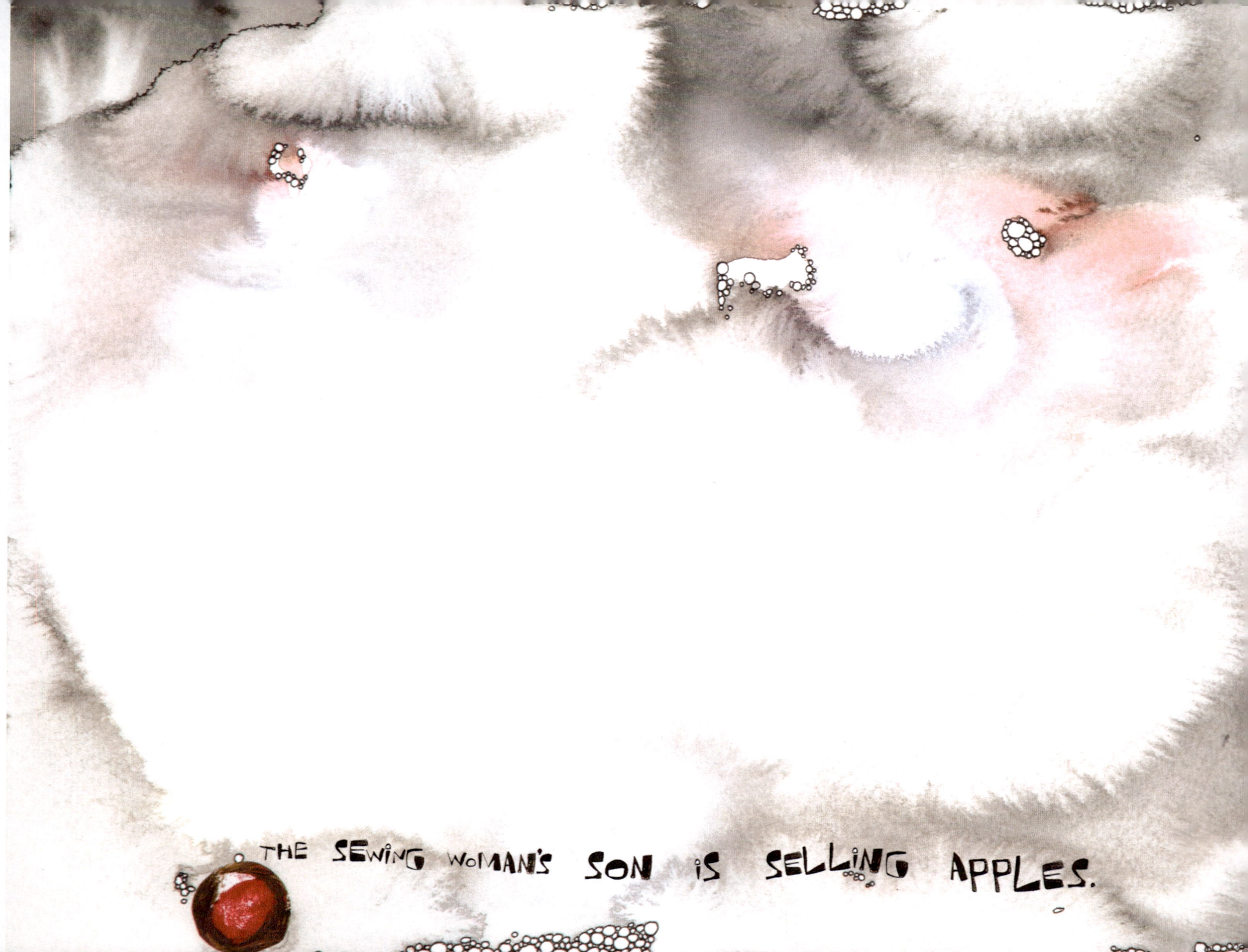

THE SEWING WOMAN'S SON IS SELLING APPLES.

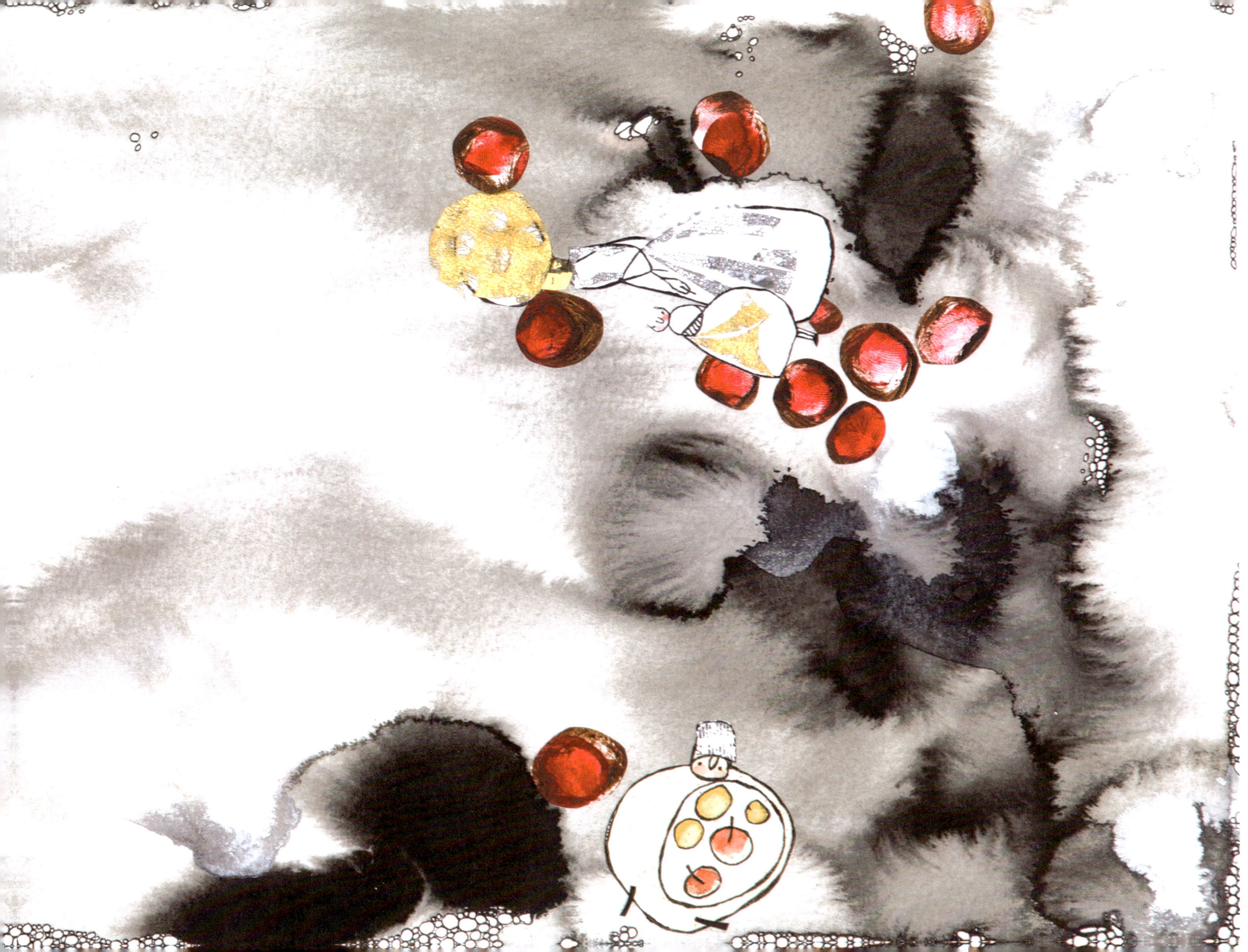

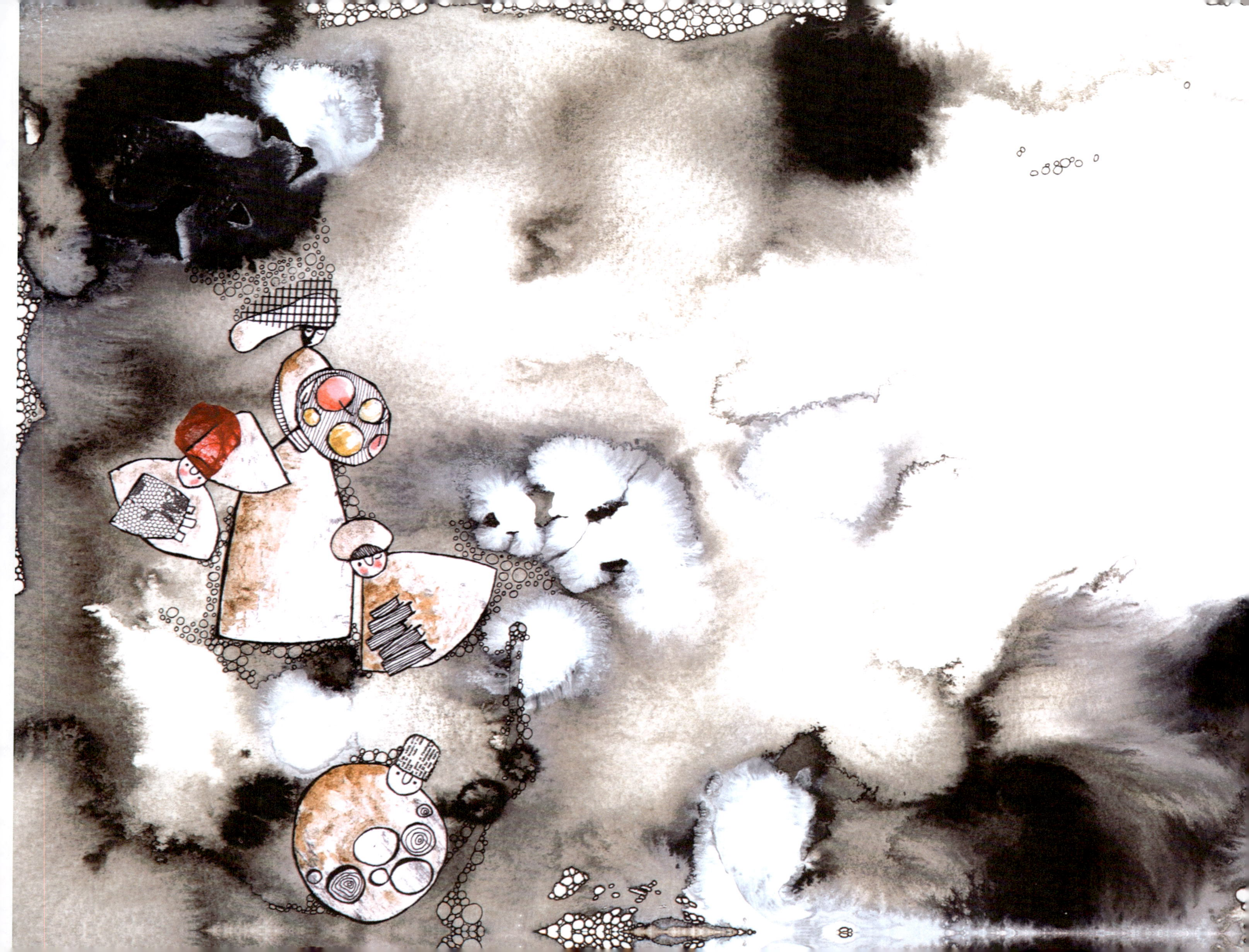

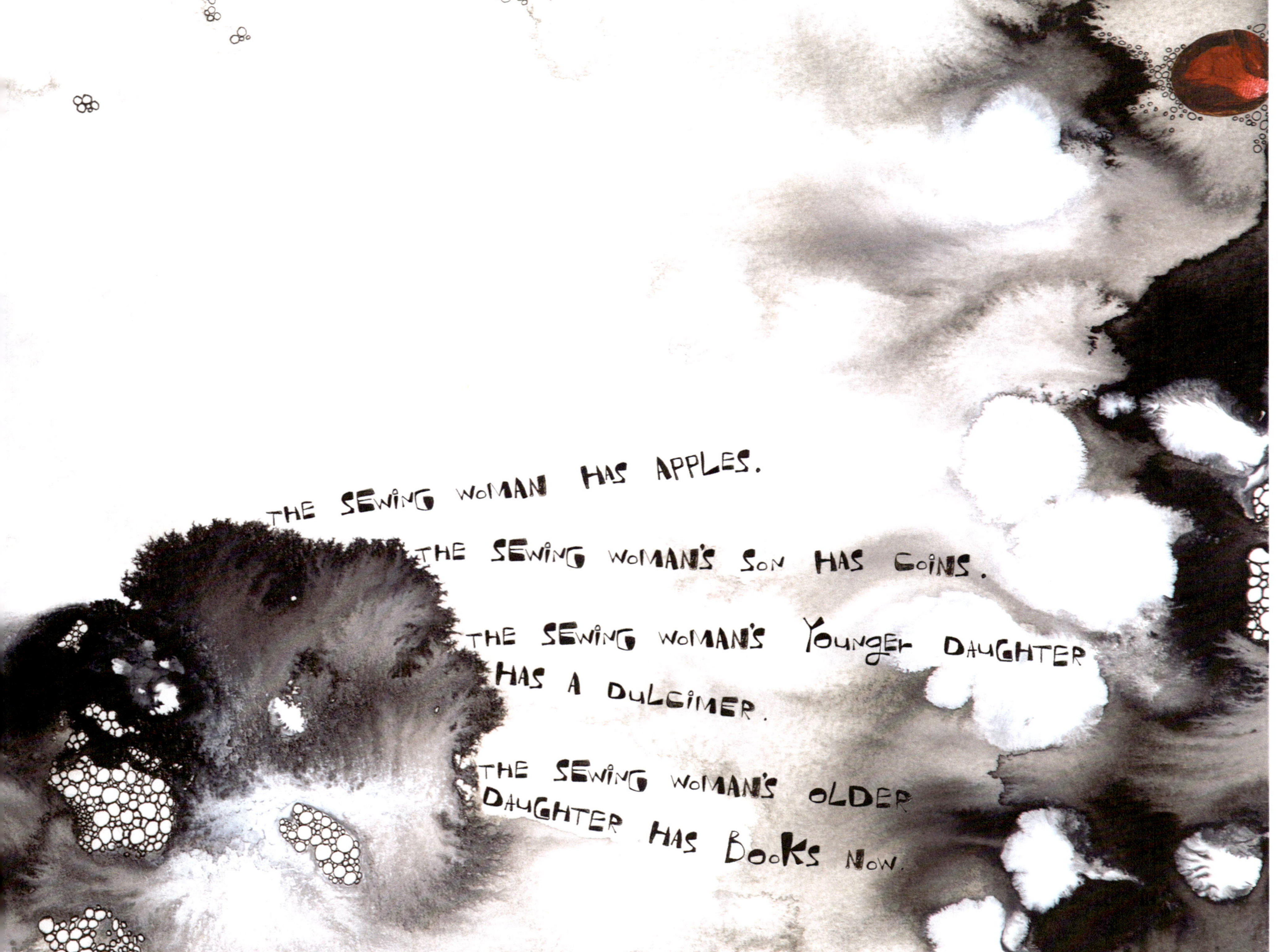

THE SEWING WOMAN HAS APPLES.
THE SEWING WOMAN'S SON HAS COINS.
THE SEWING WOMAN'S YOUNGER DAUGHTER HAS A DULCIMER.
THE SEWING WOMAN'S OLDER DAUGHTER HAS BOOKS NOW.

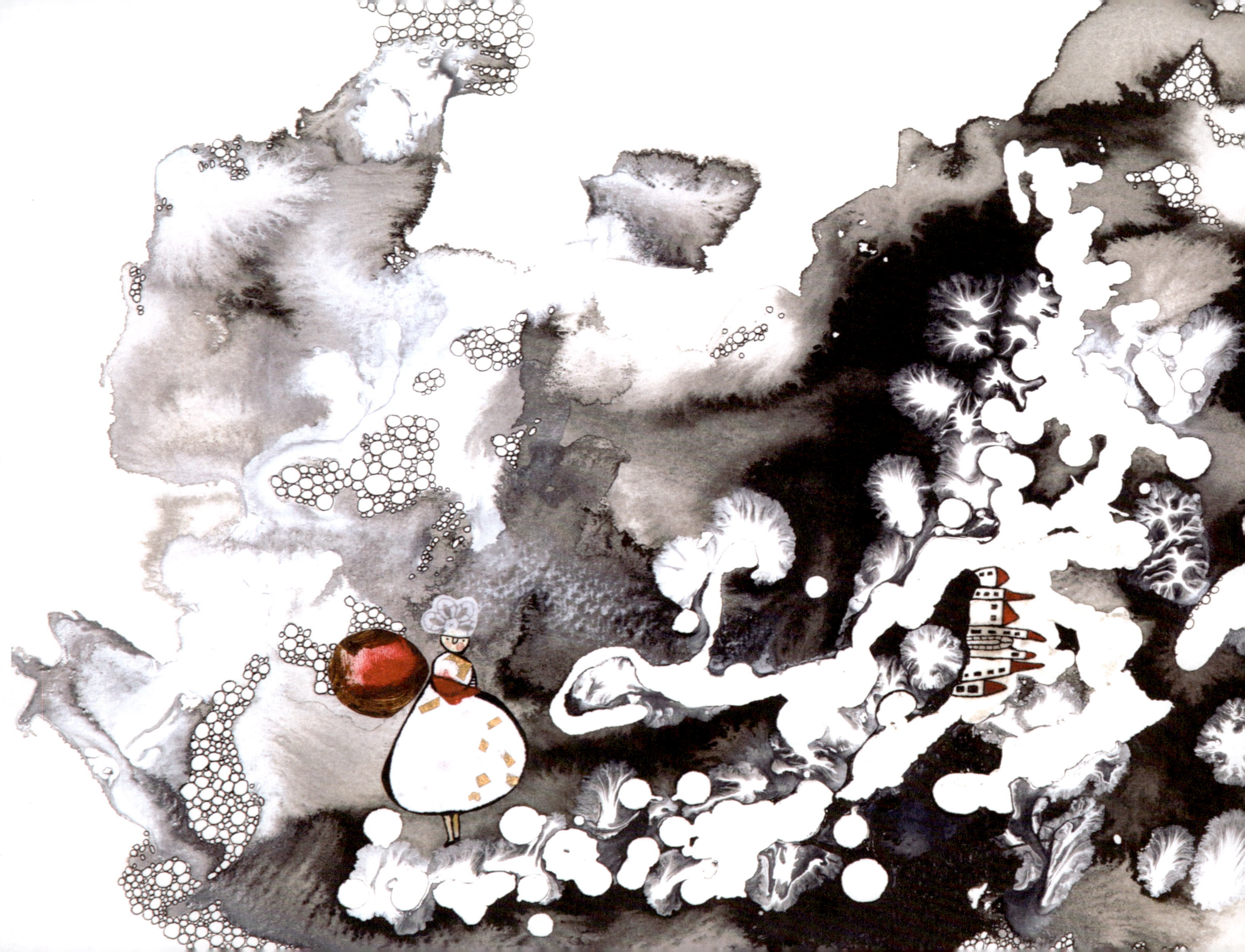

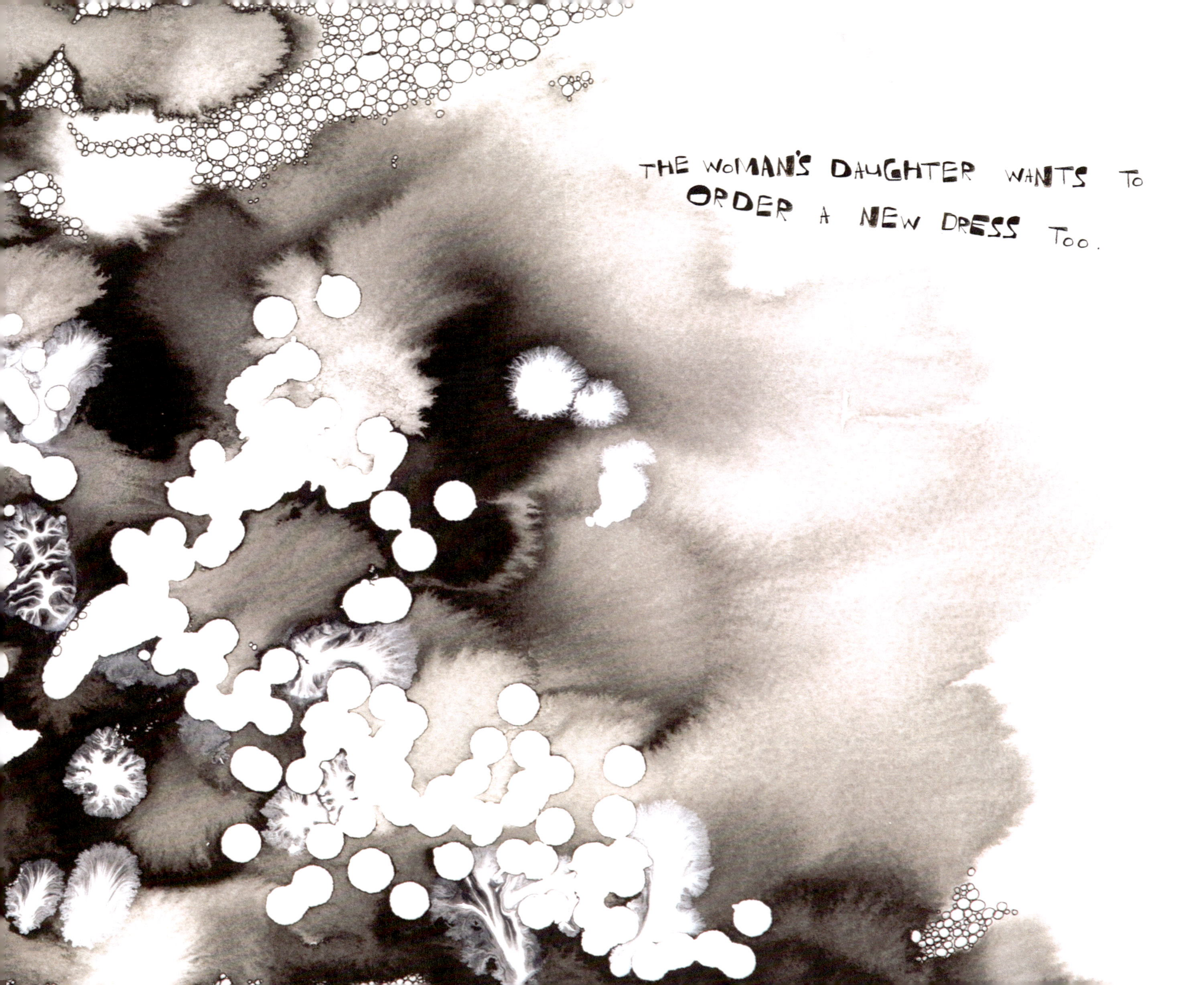

THE WOMAN'S DAUGHTER WANTS TO ORDER A NEW DRESS TOO.

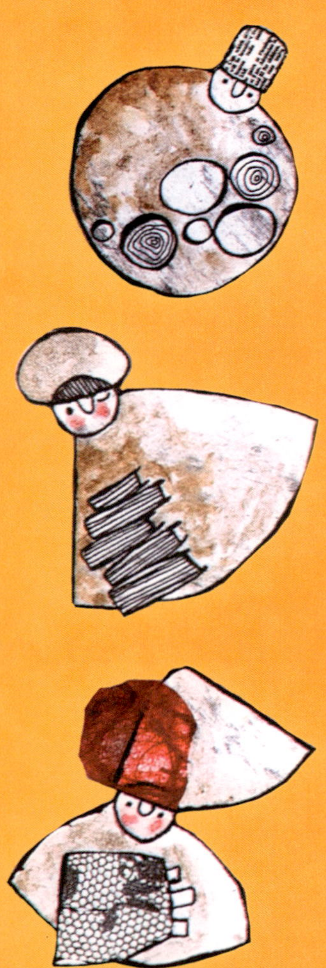

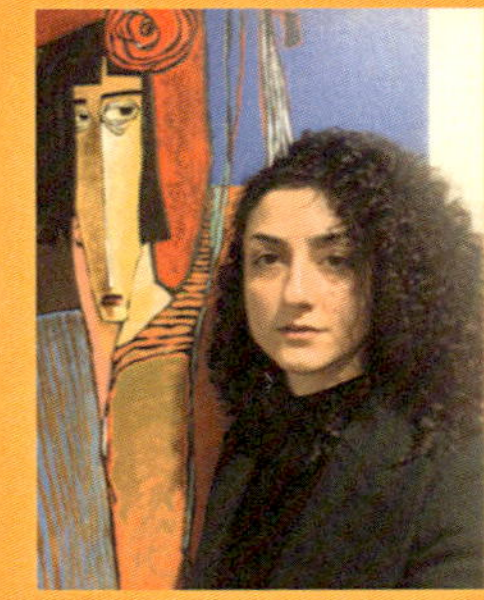

Bahar Taghiani is an illustrator and visual artist whose love for visual imagery began in early childhood. She started by creating characters out of pieces of paper, placing them in imagined stories, and bringing them to life. Today, her artworks are primarily created using mediums such as acrylic, collage, colored pencil, and watercolor, drawing inspiration from her perception of the world around her. Bahar is an award-winning artist, recognized by UNICEF for her illustration in the competition "Children on the Eve of New Year."

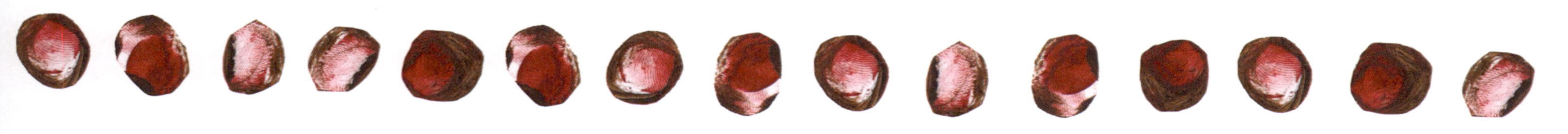

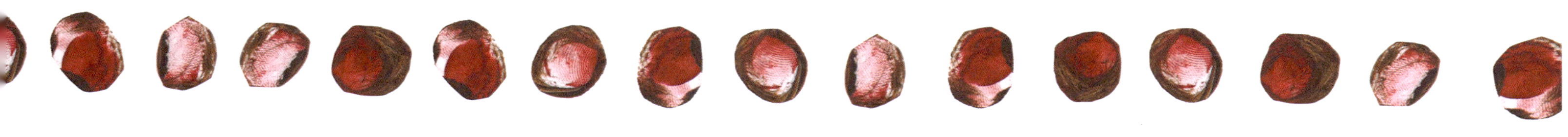

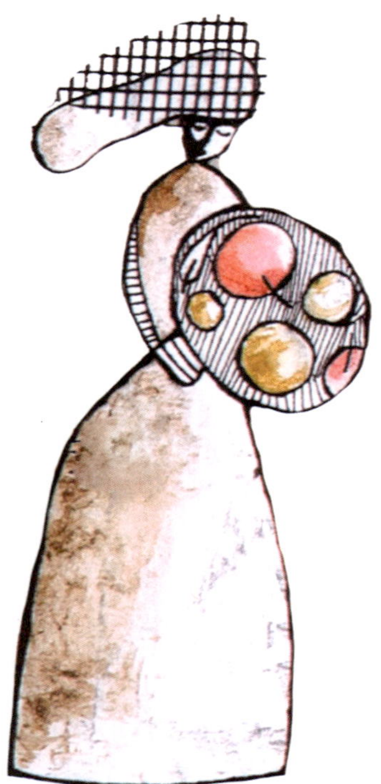